# CRICKET
## the golden age

# CRIC
## the golder

# KET
## age

**Duncan Steer**

CASSELL
ILLUSTRATED

First published in Great Britain in
2003 by Cassell Illustrated,
a division of Octopus Publishing
Group Limited
2–4 Heron Quays,
London E14 4JP

Text by Duncan Steer
Editorial, design and layout
by Essential Works

Cassell Illustrated acknowledge
the assistance provided by
Getty Images.

**getty**images

A CIP catalogue record for this
book is available from the British
Library.

ISBN 1-84403-089-X

Printed in Italy

I.   foreword 6

II.  introduction by Graham Gooch 8

III. the photographs 10

IV.  index 380

V.   photographic credits 384

VI.  acknowledgements 384

# FOREWORD

ricket is about more than mere statistics; about more even than great games and great performances. Anyone who has loved the game will have a clutch of memories related only distantly to the great events on the field, as reported in the daily press.

I have stood outside The Oval in the pouring rain on a Sunday afternoon somehow expecting that the next pitch inspection – at 5.30, say – might allow us to see ten overs' play before night sets in. I have sat among the characters in a county crowd and wondered what on earth they could possibly do for a living – and where they go in winter. I have played in a game in the dust at the side of an A-road in Pakistan and spoken to Tony Greig on a rooftop in Tangier. I have been inside a ground two hours before a Cup semi-final and taken in the slowly building atmosphere. I have had it suggested to me when I umpired 'for' a Sunday team that one should not even consider giving lbws against one's 'own' players. It happens.

You will have your own versions of these: a roster of favoured memories, punctuated by the occasional thrilling brush with celebrity. For good or ill, every day in cricket is memorable.

'Cricket: The Golden Age' is a celebration of the random reasons that make us love the game, as captured by some of the greatest photographers of the last 150 years. It is not a comprehensive history of the game's key events and star players. Indeed, there are no more than a handful of photographs of professional cricket actually being played. Great names and great events do feature, of course, but the accent is on great characters and great photography.

Photographers have always focused not just on the best players but on the biggest characters too. Maurice Tate, for example, may well have been one of the best bowlers in the world in the late 1920s, but we have included him here - three times no less - for the sheer heartiness of his approach to life and the stunts it led him towards. He balances twin girls on his shoulders while smoking a pipe. He opens a pub. He races dogs across country. We know instinctively, across the chasm of decades, that here was a man with whom we would like to have had a drink. Denis Compton, Don Bradman, Walter Hammond and Jack Hobbs feature strongly, as does Ian Botham: all men whose characters transcended their mere sporting excellence and whose celebrity took them beyond the game that had created their fame. But they appear alongside the ordinary fans and village and bomb-site players without whom the game would not exist. The game, after all, belongs to us, the supporters.

Three hundred great photographs. Some funny, some sad, some nostalgic – but all of them reflecting some part of the game's rich, but sometimes plain odd, tapestry. Bing Crosby keeping wicket? Andy Williams taking cricket lessons from Alec Stewart's dad? Eric

Morecambe turning his arm over? Snow stopping play? Snow not stopping play? It's all here.

Our collection is mainly drawn from the archives of the Fox Photos and Keystone Press picture agencies and 'Picture Post' magazine, all now owned and housed by Getty Images. Fox and Keystone photographs were used in the full range of national and international media from the early part of the 20th century. 'Picture Post', meanwhile, was published for less than 20 years – from 1938 to 1957 – but won a lasting reputation for its style of documenting everyday life in Britain, as well as news events, through great black and white photography. In addition, we have drawn on Getty's Allsport collection, which has been covering sport across the world for the last 25 years.

We take for granted now that overseas tours will be covered by a battalion of press photographers, and that action shots will be in-your-face close-ups. But even the bigger agencies were loath to send snappers on tours bookended by five-week cruises. And it was only in the 1960s that technology ushered in the modern age of sports photography – and a morning spent looking at the distant shots from the boundaries used by newspapers before then is enough to remind you exactly how far sports photography has come. On the other hand, the imagination and technique behind the great documentary and portrait photography of that previous age can make you wonder if something has not been lost as well as won. DUNCAN STEER

# INTRODUCTION by Graham Gooch

**E**very weekend, our whole family used to go and watch my dad play for the East Ham Corinthians. My mum would take the picnic – she had one of those old hampers, with plastic plates strapped inside the lid – and I'd split the afternoon between watching the game and pestering the players to throw balls to me outside the boundary.

All week, I looked forward to those Sundays. And all summer, I looked forward to the final game of the season, which involved a coach trip to Clacton-on-Sea. They had a decent ground and their side was a bit stronger than ours was. It'd only take a couple of hours to get there, but it felt like we were going to the other end of England. On the way back, we'd stop and have something to eat, all the men would have a beer and we'd get home at midnight. For a little kid, it was fantastic.

Some of us go on to play at a high level and some stay playing in the parks, but I've never forgotten that we all start playing because we love the game and the whole atmosphere around it. The pictures in this book capture some of that unique atmosphere and bring to mind for me not just my own early days in the game and some of the great players I played alongside, but also many of the great characters I knew only as selectors and ex-players. On the morning of my first

Test in 1975, Sir Len Hutton, who was one of the selectors, came over to wish me good luck and asked me if I'd ever played against Australia before. I didn't know what to say – I'd played for the MCC against Australia only the previous week, and Len had been the man who had picked me then as well.

The tales that came down to us from previous generations suggested a different kind of world. Sir Colin Cowdrey liked to tell me how he would play nine holes of golf the morning before a Test match. Mickey Stewart told me that because the professionals and amateurs used to change in different rooms, the great Surrey captain of the 1950s, Stuart Surridge, would often dispense his post-match thoughts by telephone between the two.

Even when I started playing for Essex in the early 1970s, things were pretty carefree. Our star overseas player Kenny McEwan's sponsored car for the season was the Transit van we used to lug the kit around the country. Our captain, Keith Fletcher, would happily call a player away from Sunday lunch to drive to the other end of the country in an apparent emergency – only to make him twelfth man. Once, Keith Pont cut out some work in the field by riding a spectator's bike round the boundary from long leg to long leg in between overs.

The game is more professional now and, unfortunately, that doesn't always mix with the characters in the game. I don't know how much chance I'd get now to do the bowling impressions that I did at the end of a dying Test in 1979. I did Tony Greig's run-up

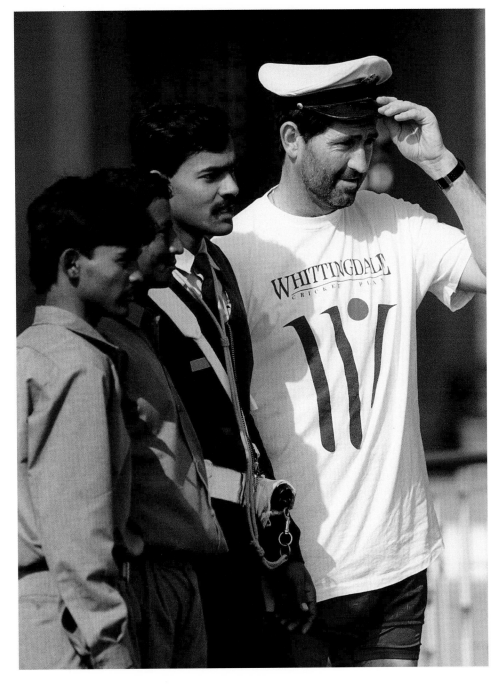

and Bob Willis'. I did Chris Old, as well – I just ran up and acted like my back had gone and the boys had to carry me off. When we were in India in 1982, I decided to liven things up by impersonating Dilip Doshi, their left-arm spinner and master time-waster. Every ball, he would move a fielder six inches to the left or six inches to the right. I borrowed some glasses from a bloke in the crowd and did my impression of him, doing some left-arm spin with these glasses on. I think I still hold the record as the only bowler to bowl left- and right-handed in the same Test.

As a player, you never lose sight of exactly how much the game means to people. At Essex, our two biggest fans were probably Maurice and Elaine Berkeley. They were both in their 80s and they came to every single game, home and away. They became close to the team and took us out for dinner, with a strict hierarchy emerging as to who was asked first: the great stylist McEwan, the skipper and David Acfield were at the top, invited out for a slap-up dinner at a country house hotel on every single trip; for middle-rankers like myself, the chance of an invite was 50-50; then there was the cattle class category – Keith Pont, Ray East, Brian Hardie, they knew who they were – who'd be lucky to get the nod from the judge maybe once a season. It became a big joke in the dressing room. They'd write long letters to us, too. They were great people.

That's what cricket people are like – they build their lives around the game because they love it. And we haven't even mentioned the supporters club

coach – a load of guys ready to get up at two in the morning and travel for eight hours to Taunton, only to find out it's going to rain all day. This is a book about those fans who sit in the rain and about teams like the East Ham Corinthians, as well as about some of the fun and the dramas those of us lucky enough to play the game at the highest level have been a part of. For me, these photographs evoke great memories, not only of international cricket, but also of starting out and of how cricket is enjoyed by players and spectators all over the world, at every level.

Lunchtime in the City of London. October
1945. Photograph by Harry Todd/Fox

Denis Compton and Bill Edrich leave the field after clinching England's first Ashes win since 1933. August 1953. Photographer not known

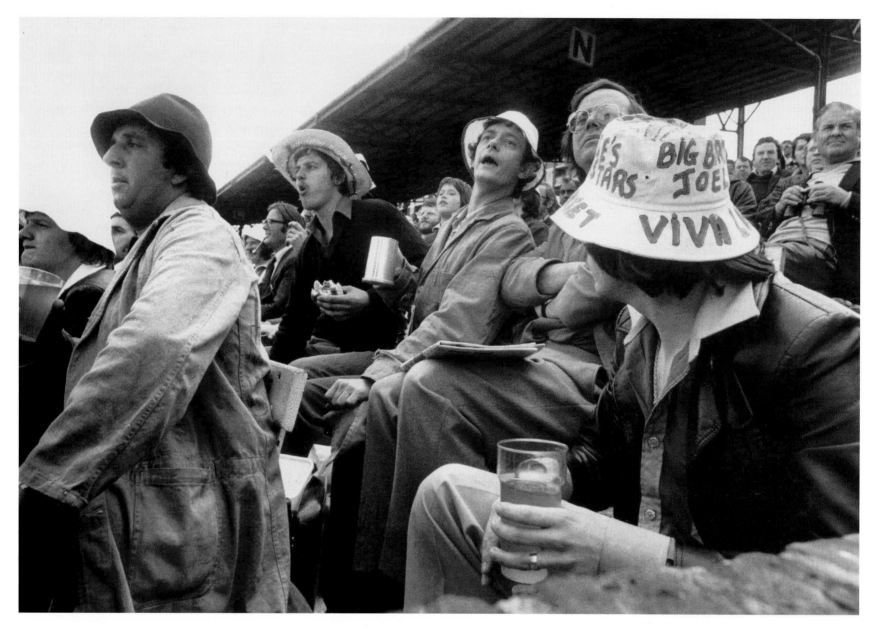

Somerset fans at Lord's for the Gillette Cup semi-final against Middlesex. They saw their team win by seven wickets on the way to the county's first-ever trophy. August 1979. Photographer not known

Opposite: Mick Jagger returns to his seat at the final England versus Australia Test at the Oval. August 1972. Photographer not known

**Warwickshire train for the new season. April 1938.** Photograph by George Hales/Fox

Sussex and England stalwart Maurice Tate takes on the Brighton Foot Beagles in a race across the countryside, reason not known. January 1937.
Photograph by William G Vanderson/Fox

Tony Lock on tour with England in South Africa. He takes his dartboard with him wherever he goes. December 1956. Photographer not known

Opposite: Groundsman 'Bosser' Martin with his heavy roller at the Oval, after England have hit a record 903 in their first innings on the pitch he prepared. August 1938. Photographer not known

The England tour party celebrate their return from a 2-0 Ashes victory by going into the recording studio. Commentator Brian Johnston (left) co-wrote 'The Ashes Song', which fails to trouble the chart scorers. April 1971. Photograph by Ian Shaw/Keystone

Crowds gather for the opening of England's Jack Hobbs'
sports shop in Fleet Street. 1925. Photographer not known

HOBBS LTD.
SURREY XI.

BRISTOL
OBSERVER

JACK HOBBS
SPORTS OUTFITTERS
Fleet 59 Street

58 Dersey

Dersey's Sale
SWEEPING
REDUCTIONS

Dersey's Sale
SWEEPING
REDUCTIONS

Dersey's
Sale

10s Quality
BEDFORD
CORD
TUNIC
S

Half
Price
DAY

Arul Mary, 23, prepares the Colombo Oval for the Ceylon versus MCC game. She is believed to be the world's only 'groundswoman'. October 1954. Photographer not known

Opposite: Mr and Mrs Cochrane making bats at their family firm in Lewes. She claimed to be Britain's only lady batmaker. 1951. Photographer not known

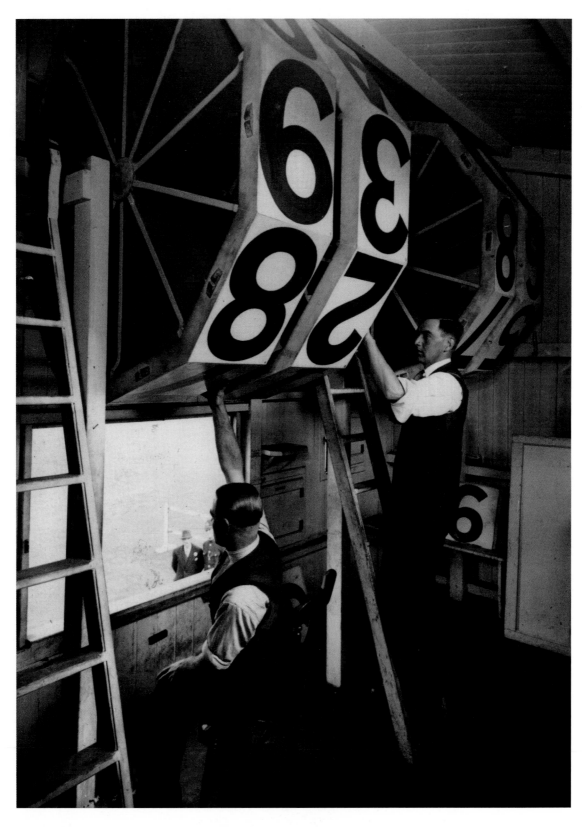

Inside the Trent Bridge scoreboard. 1935. Photographer not known

Opposite: Kenton Cricket Club scoreboard. Circa 1952. Photograph by George Douglas

**Diehard. May 1924.** Photograph by Sharples/Topical Press

England's Colin Milburn recovers in hospital after losing an eye in a car crash. He tells reporters he intends to carry on playing. May 1969. Photographer not known

Opposite: A fortnight later, Milburn commentates on the first England versus West Indies Test for the BBC. June 1969. Photographer not known

A futuristic turf-piercing machine goes on display at a show organised by the National Association of Groundsmen at Hurlingham, London. November 1957. Photographer not known

Opposite: Demonstrating a turf-drying machine at the National Association of Groundsmen's annual show at Hurlingham. October 1954. Photographer not known

Jack Hobbs chooses willow for his bats. March 1922. Photographer not known

Queueing spectators before the deciding Ashes Test at the Oval pass the time with a game of cards.
August 1926. Photographer not known

23 years after his last appearance for England, Harold Larwood works on deliveries for Pepsi in Sydney. 1956. Photograph by Dennis Rowe

Opposite: Having opted out of playing against Australia in the return series a year after Bodyline, Douglas Jardine queues outside the Oval for the last Test of the series. The ex-skipper commentated on the match. 1934. Photographer not known

Rodney Marsh, Australian wicket-keeper. March 1977. Photographer not known

Fred Trueman relaxes after becoming the first cricketer to take 300 Test wickets. His four-wicket haul against Australia has taken him to 301. August 1964.
Photographer not known

HIRE A CUSHION FOR COMFORT
only 6D
LEAVE ON SEAT AFTER USE

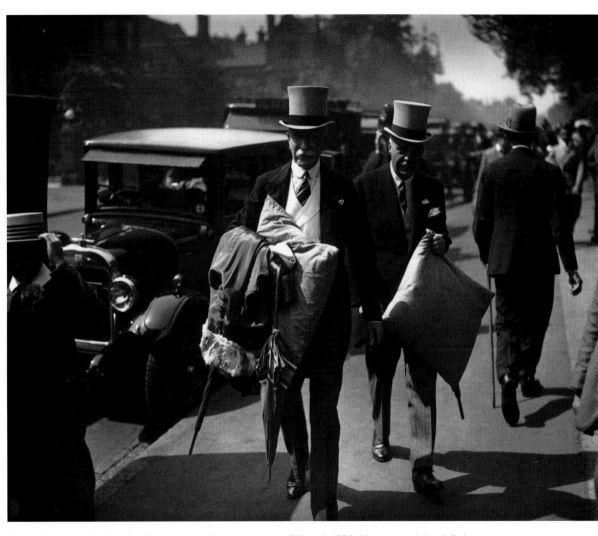

Spectators arrive for the Eton versus Harrow game of March 1932. Photograph by J. Gaiger

Opposite: A full house of hats at Headingley for the England versus Australia game. July 1930. Photographer not known

**A day-night game at Sydney Cricket Ground. February 1985.** Photograph by Adrian Murrell/Allsport

Middlesex take the field in the first-ever women's county match, against Kent at Chiswick House, Middlesex. May 1934. **Photograph by J.A. Hampton**

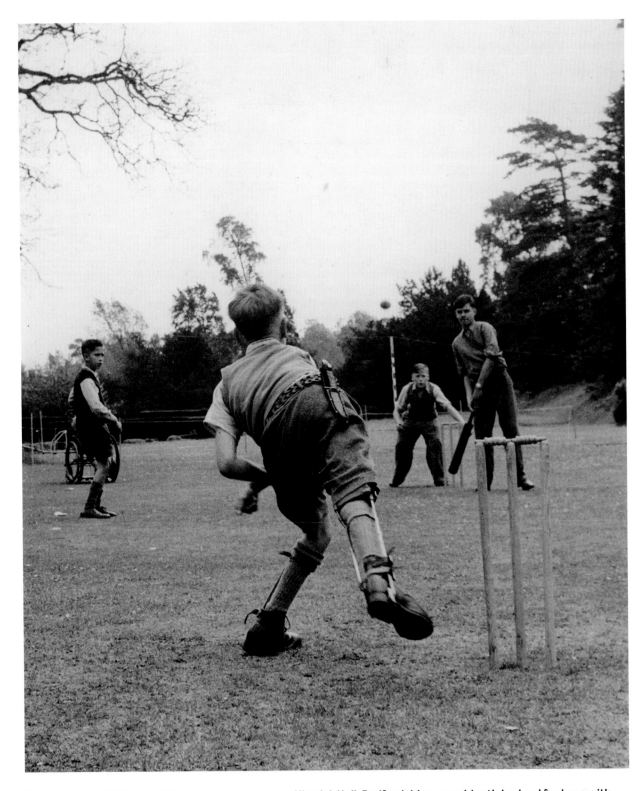

Twelve-year-old Tim Cowell bowls during a game at Hinwick Hall, Bedfordshire, a residential school for boys with muscular distrophy. May 1956. Photograph by John Pratt

Opposite: Lunch hour cricket on the bombsites behind London's Moorgate station. April 1950.
Photographer not known

Douglas Jardine (left) presents the County Cricketers Billiards Championships trophy to Leicestershire's Ewart Astill (right). Runner-up Alf Gover is in the middle. January 1936.
Photograph by David Savill/Topical Press

Opposite: Footballer, cricketer, politician and polymath C.B. Fry – now commander of a Royal Navy training ship – inspects a model of himself as a young man. June 1950.
Photographer not known

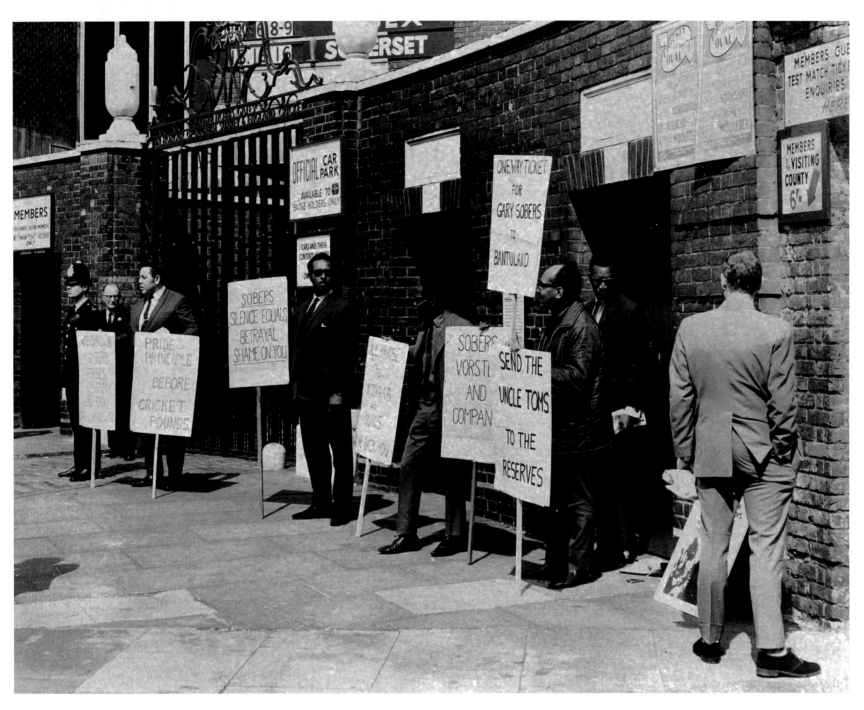

Anti-apartheid protestors outside the Oval. 1960. Photographer not known

Opposite: Graffiti on the scoreboard at Bristol, ahead of the proposed South African tour. January 1970. Photographer not known

Guests play cricket on the lawn at the annual Buckingham Palace Garden Party. July 1958. Photograph by Hales

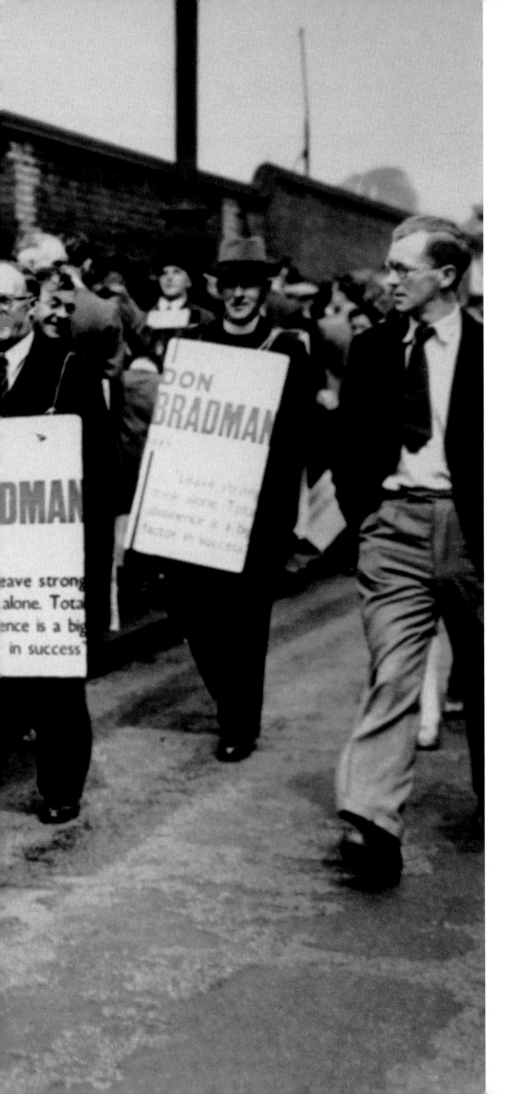

Anti-drink clergymen canvass support before an Ashes Test.
Circa 1948. Photographer not known

57

Don Bradman walks out to bat at Headingley. August 1938. Photographer not known

Opposite: Bradman carried off after injuring his foot at the Oval. August 1938. Photographer not known

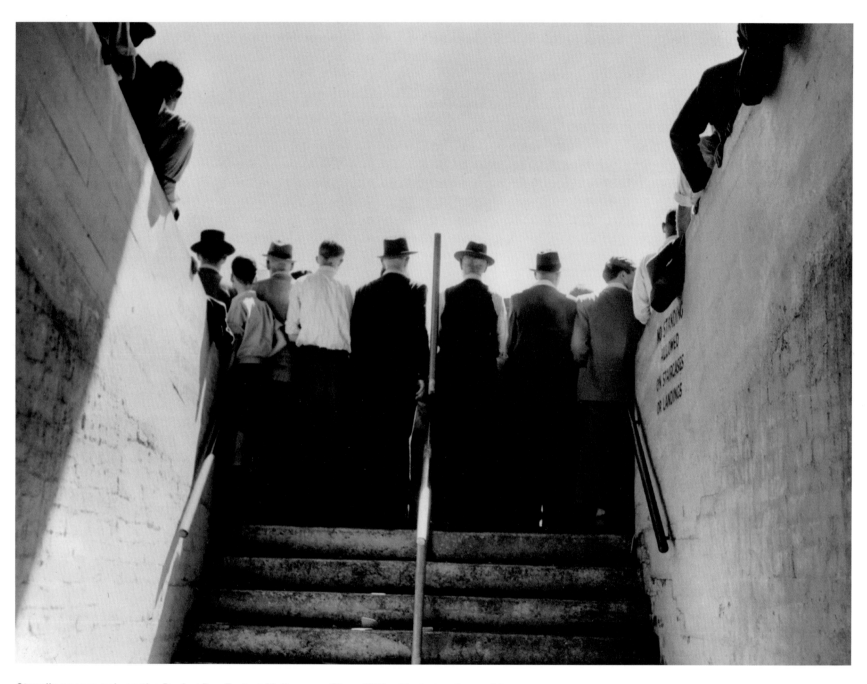

Standing room only at the Boxing Day Test at Melbourne. Circa 1950s. Photographer not known

Len Hutton leaves the field after his record-breaking 364 not out against Australia at the Oval. June 1938. Photographer not known

Making inroads into the 50-foot long and 3-foot deep pile of beer cans left at the Sydney Cricket Ground after the third Australia versus West Indies Test. January 1969. Photographer not known

Laid-back cricket fans in New Zealand. December 1953. Photograph by Thurston Hopkins

Opposite: A precarious view of the Oval. Circa 1976. Photographer not known

The captains examine the pitch before the Leicestershire versus South Africa game. May 1924. Photograph by Kirby

Don Bradman (left) and Wally Hammond toss before the Ashes Test at the Oval, with groundsman 'Bosser' Martin looking on. August 1938.
Photographer not known

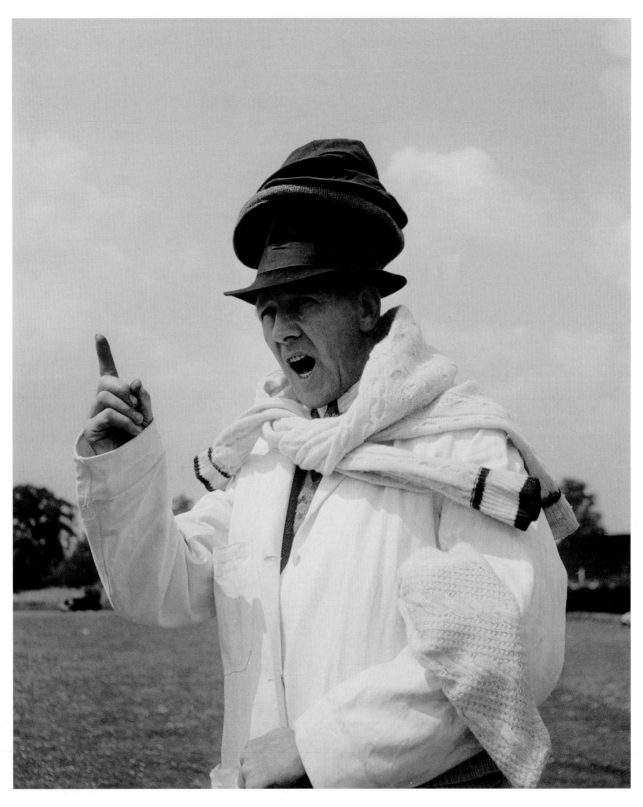

Umpire, Amersham Hill, Buckinghamshire. June 1949. Photograph by Chris Ware
Opposite: Fans at Old Trafford make a boater tower. July 1938. Photographer not known

Getting ready for the new season at Lillywhite, Frowd and Co., kit manufacturers, London. Circa 1930. Photographer not known

Jack Hobbs opens the Hobbs Gates at the Oval, on the first day of his last season of first-class cricket. May 1934. Photographer not known

Following pages, left: Mixed reactions in the crowd as West Indies' Conrad Hunte drops a catch in the final Test against England at the Oval. August 1963. Photographer not known

Following pages, right: West Indies fans celebrate a 158-run win over England in the first Test at the Oval. August 1973. Photographer not known

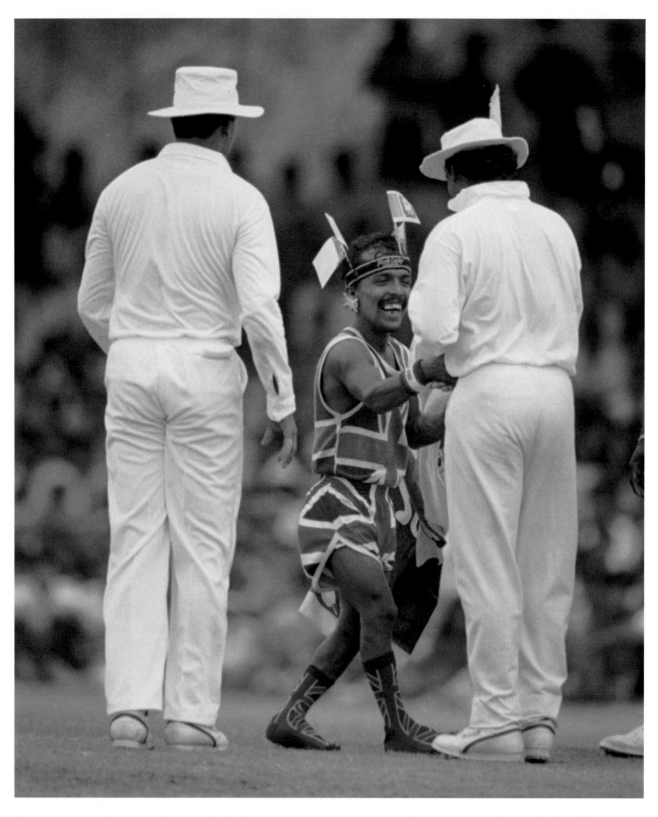

A lone member of the crowd invades the field during a one-day international between Sri Lanka and England. March 1993. Photograph by Richard Saker

Opposite: England women's captain Rachel Heyhoe comes up against comedy stalwart Cardew 'The Cad' Robinson of the Lord's Taverners, ahead of a charity game. June 1967. Photographer not known

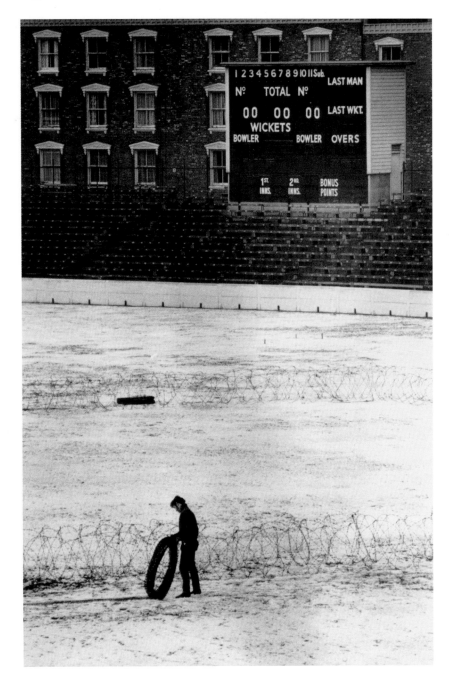

Protecting the Oval pitch from potential damage from anti-apartheid protestors ahead of the planned South African tour. February 1970.
Photographer not known

Opposite: The Oval as a prisoner of war camp. November 1944.
Photographer not known

The Indian party ready for home at London's Victoria station at the end of their first Test tour of England. September 1932.
Photographer not known

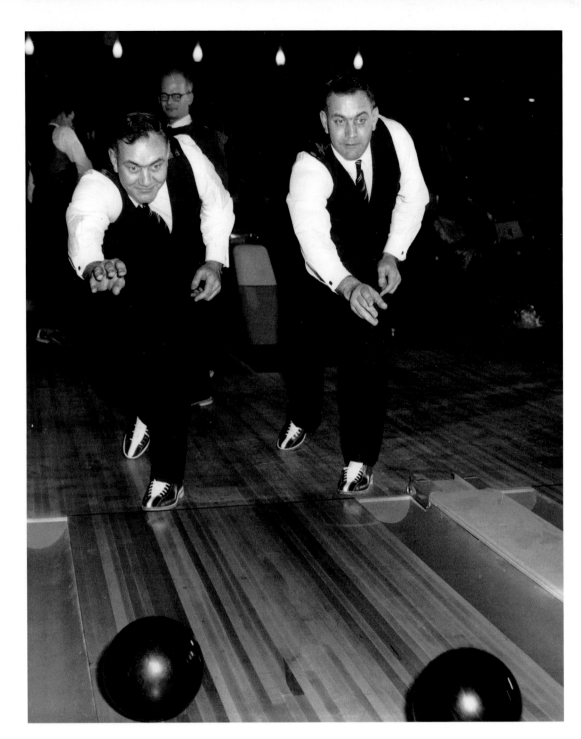

Alec and Eric Bedser try underarm bowling at England's first Ten-Pin Bowling Centre at Stamford Hill, London. January 1960. Photographer not known

Opposite: Eric Morecambe and Graham Hill bowl in a temporary indoor net at London's Café Royal. The batsmen are winners of a street cricket competition organised by the Lord's Taverners. April 1973. Photographer not known

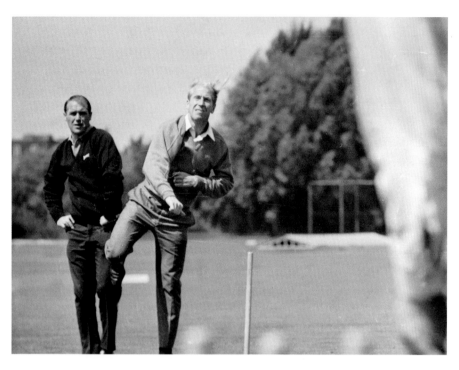

Bobby Charlton turns his arm over as England's footballers play cricket the day before the 1966 World Cup final. July 1966. Photograph by Terry Fincher

Right: Chelsea manager, England World Cup hero (and former Essex cricketer) Geoff Hurst takes on the West Indies at Stamford Bridge, with former Antigua footballer Viv Richards behind the timbers. The tourists are about to take on Essex in the first floodlit cricket game to be staged at the ground. August 1980. Photographer not known

Bob Willis, Derek Randall, Mike Hendrick, David Gower and Ian Botham prepare for the forthcoming Ashes series. October 1978. Photographer not known

Batting practice at the first-ever residential training course for cricket coaches. January 1950.
Photographer not known

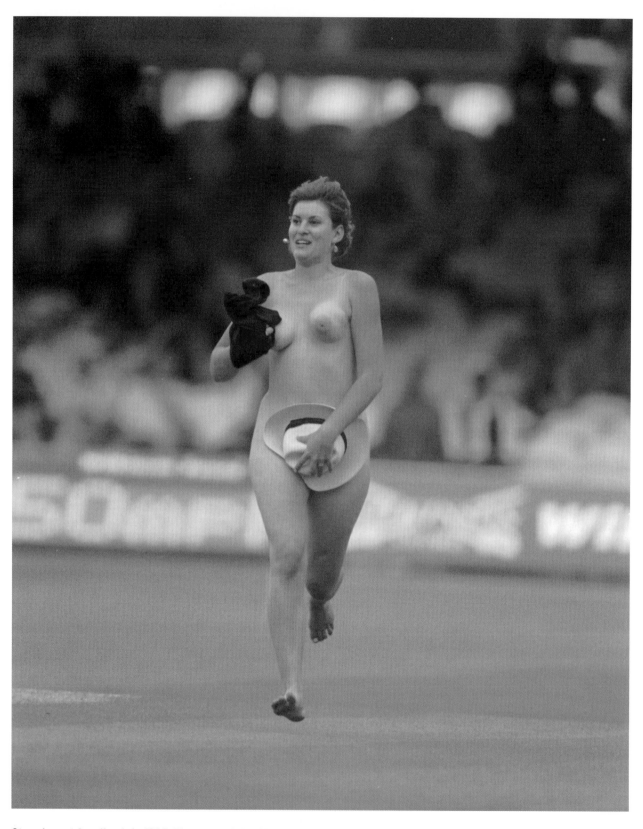

**Streaker at Lord's. July 1996.** Photograph by Allsport

**Opposite: A member of the Addlestone women's team drops a catch. 1924.** Photographer not known

Australian captain Bill Lawry meets the press on the tarmac at Heathrow. April 1968.
Photograph by Dennis Oulds

England Test player (and future captain of India) The Nawab of Pataudi, Senior, puts his best foot forward. 1937. Photographer not known

Opposite: The Duke of Edinburgh plays across the line. June 1949. Photographer not known

Wood Green Rotary Club turn back the clock for their game with the local Chamber of Commerce. 1933. Photographer not known

Local boys consider the crowd queuing for the Eton-Harrow game at Lord's. 1937. Photograph by Jimmy Sime

A cricketer has her cigarette lit before a practice session. May 1935. Photographer not known

Opposite: Errol Holmes gets ready to take the field at Penshurst Castle, Kent. August 1934. Photographer not known

The crowd invade the Oval after the final Ashes Test. Australia had won the series 2–1. August 1930. Photographer not known

Opposite: Packing balls at a workshop in Norwood Junction, London. February 1936. Photograph by Harry Todd

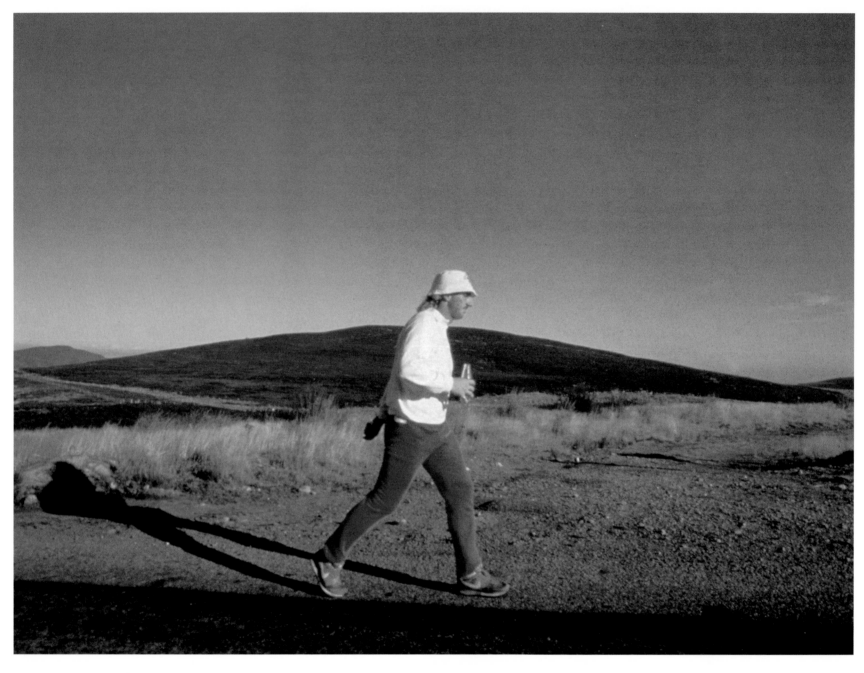

Ian Botham en route from John O'Groats to Land's End, on the first of his marathon walks for charity. This one raised over a million pounds.
November 1985. Photograph by Adrian Murrell

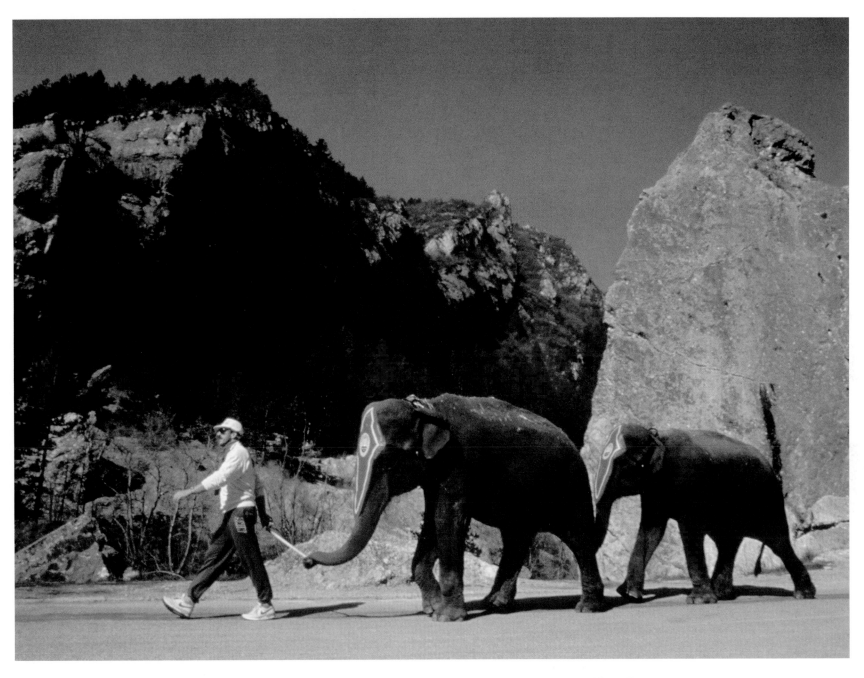

Botham in the footsteps of Hannibal, leading elephants across the Alps, for charity. 1988. Photograph by Adrian Murrell

England wicket-keeper Alan Knott prepares for the 1970/71 tour of Australia at The Valley, home of Charlton Athletic. October 15 1970. Photographer: Dennis Oulds

Opposite: England's Mary Johnson in catching practice. May 1951. Photograph by Bert Hardy

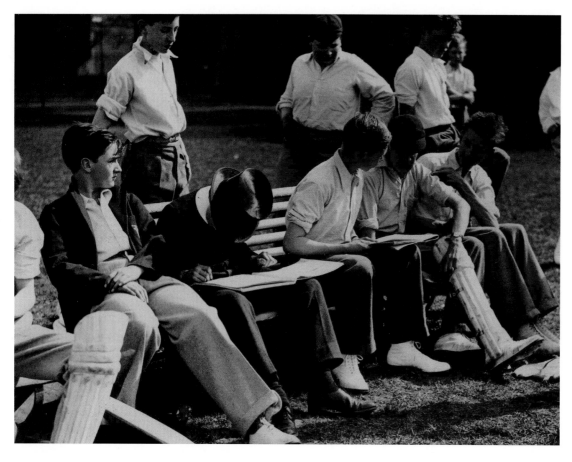

Keeping score at a Westminster School game. May 1938. Photographer not known

Opposite: The calm before the storm – a lone spectator at the first Test of the 1932–33 Ashes series, in Sydney. December 1932. Photographer not known

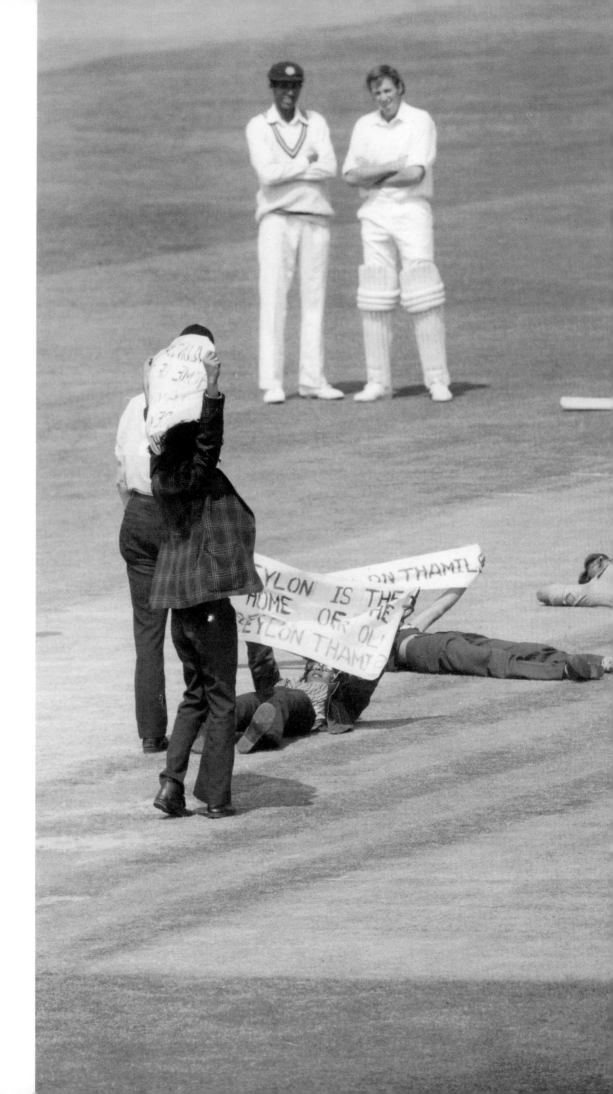

Tamil protestors stop play in Sri Lanka's World
Cup game with Australia at the Oval. June 1975.
Photographer not known

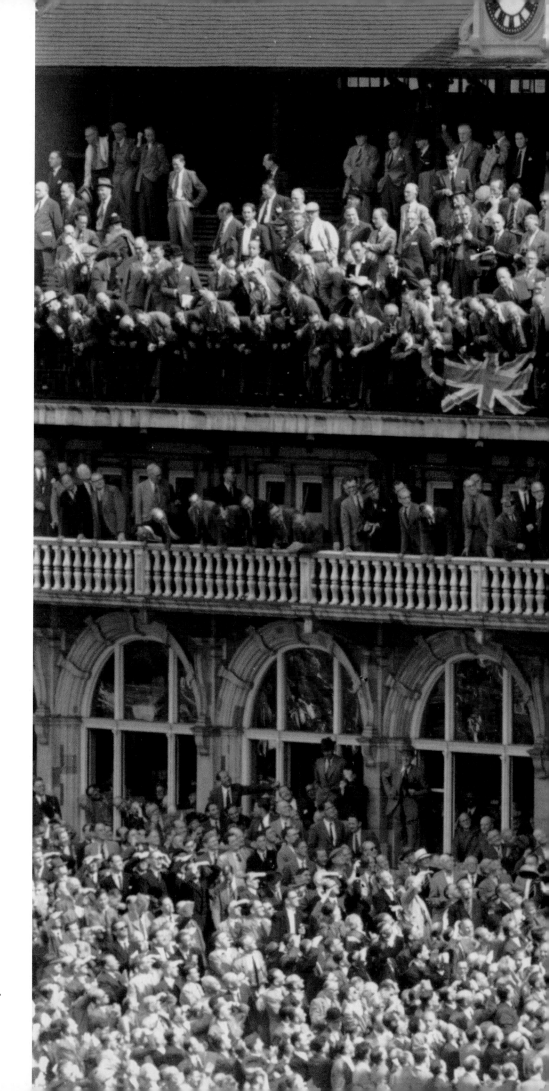

England captain Len Hutton salutes the crowd at the Oval after England regain the Ashes for the first time in 19 years. August 1953. Photographer not known

W.G. Grace. Circa 1890. Photographer not known

Opposite: W.G.'s funeral. October 1915. Photographer not known

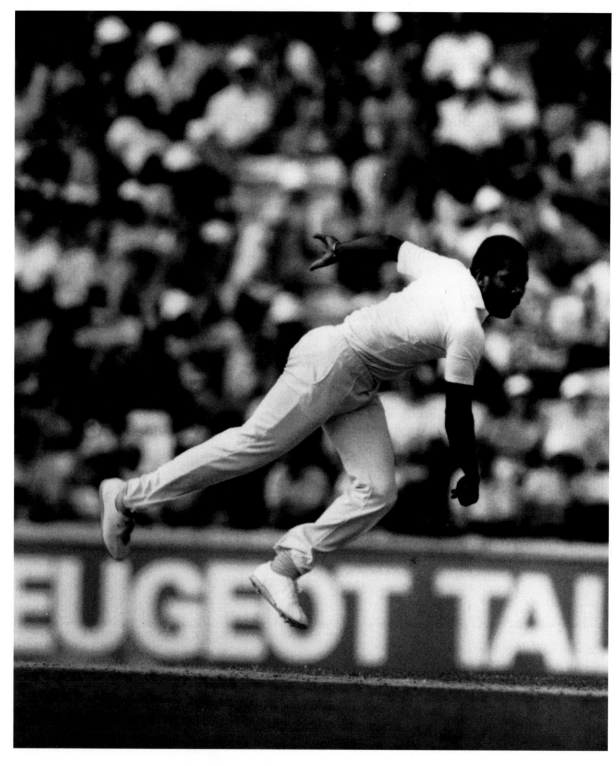

Malcolm Marshall in full flight. August 1984. Photographer not known

Opposite: Ship's cook Michael Angelow becomes the first man to streak at Lord's. He won £25 from a bet with friends – but was fined £25 by magistrates. August 1975. Photographer not known

Bringing in the harvest at Witham, Essex, where hundreds of acres are devoted to growing willow trees exclusively for cricket bat manufacturing. Each tree produces 20 bats. January 1936. Photographer not known

Following pages: The local hunt interrupts a New Year's Day match on Broadhalfpenny Down at Hambledon, the birthplace of the game. Date not known. Photographer not known

England's fancy dress party in Delhi. Boycott (left) appears as Ranjitsinjhi – Botham, apparently, appears as Boycott himself! December 1981.
Photographer not known

Opposite: Fancy dress champion Godfrey Evans, as Carmen Miranda. October 1950. Photographer not known

Graham Gooch takes tea in India. 1993. Photograph by Chris Cole

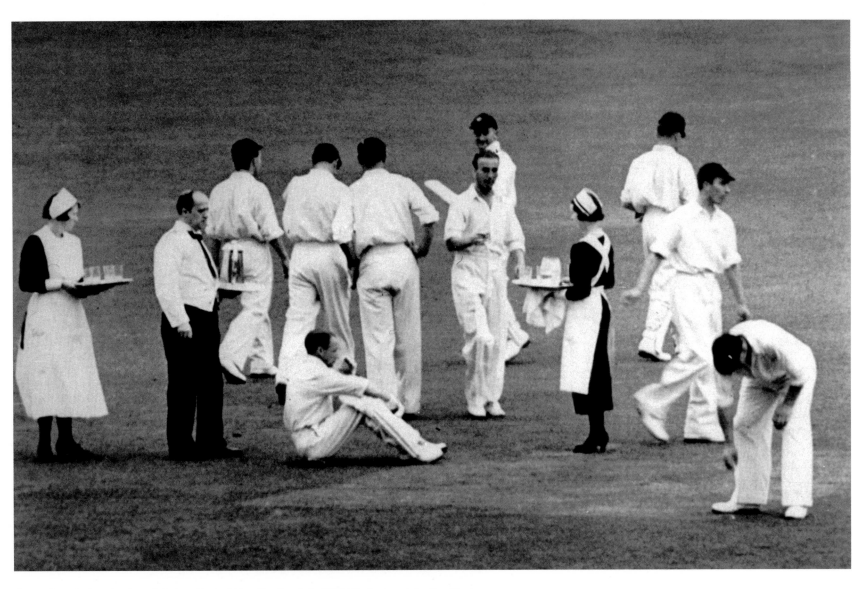

Ceasefire during the fourth Ashes Test at Headingley. July 1938. Photograph by Fox Photos

The Women's Cricket Association ready for play at Cobham, Surrey. May 1934. Photographer not known

Opposite: Making up before going out to bat. April 1932. Photographer not known

A group of strikers from the Association of Cricket Ball Makers, outside the headquarters of Duke and Sons, Kent. April 1914. Photographer not known

Two American sailors play a table cricket game on Bournemouth
Pier. September 1952. Photograph by Fred Morley

Len Hutton and actor Jack Warner in front of the camera during filming of Terrence Rattigan's 'The Final Test'. November 1952. Photograph by William Vanderson

The Nawab of Pataudi, Junior, of Sussex and India, in Brighton. 1961. Photographer not known

The Cricket Council meet to discuss South Africa's
controversial tour of England. January 1969.
Photographer not known

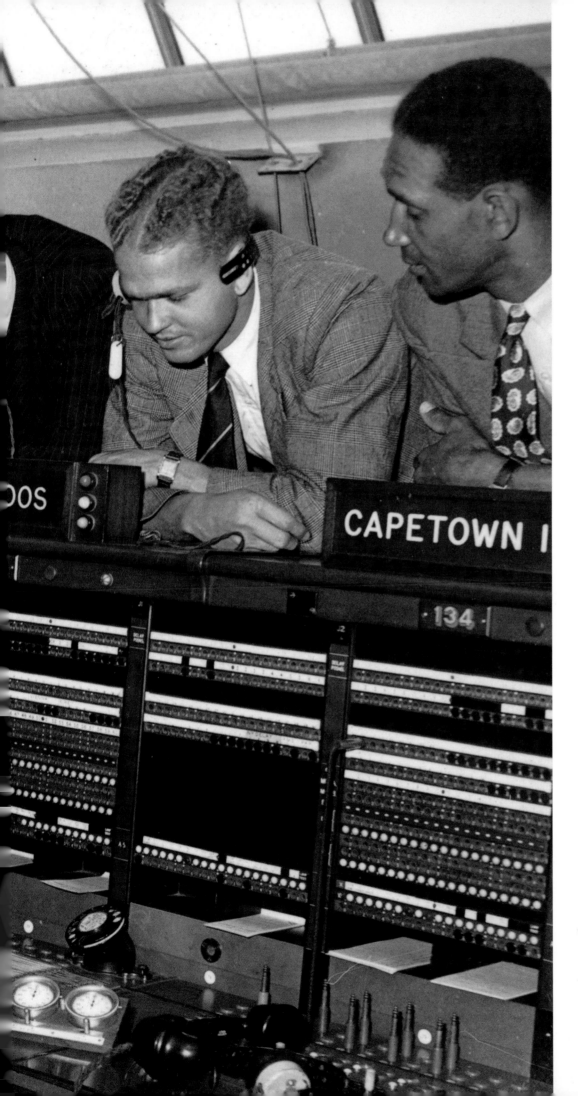

West Indies players call home from London's International Exchange, with news of their 3–1 win over England. Left to right: Everton Weekes, Clyde Walcott, team captain John Goddard, Foffie Williams and Hophnie Johnson. August 1950.

Photograph by Mrs Warren

Hanging up the finished 'quilts', or cores, of the ball to dry. Circa 1950s. Photographer not known

Opposite: Frank 'Typhoon' Tyson, believed by many to be the fastest English bowler since the Second World War, shortly after his call-up to the Test side. 1954. Photographer not known

The Parsi party for the tour of England. They were the first team of Indians to play overseas. 1886. Photograph from the Anandji Dossa Collection

Surrey unveil their new sponsor. 1975. Photographer not known

Following pages: England captain Wally Hammond gets ready to bat for his county, Gloucestershire at Bristol. 1946. Photograph by Charles Hewitt

The Rev W.P. McCormick hits out in a Bank Holiday game against a team of nurses at St Martin's-in-the-Fields church, Trafalgar Square. August 1936. Photograph by Reg Speller

Three England captains take centre stage at a wedding. Colin Cowdrey (centre) is the groom, Peter May (right) best man – with middle-order bat and future Bishop of Liverpool David Sheppard (left) officiating. September 1956. Photographer not known

Opposite: The Rev J. Martin of Itchingfield, in the dressing room before the 'Church Times' cup final between Chichester and Sheffield, at Southgate CC. Note changing hooks full of dog collars. September 1955. Photographer not known

Durham's David Boon finds the start of the season delayed by snow. April 1999. Photograph by Stu Forster

The Actors XI's opening batsmen – Edward Harben and Jack Livesey – walk to the wicket for the annual Actors versus Musicians match. 1938.
Photographer not known

England cricketers on board ship at Liverpool, en route to their tour of ...
America. September 1859. Photographer not known

Fred Trueman makes a guest appearance (playing an ex-England quick bowler called E.C. Egan) in 'Dad's Army' episode, The Test. 1970. Photographer not known

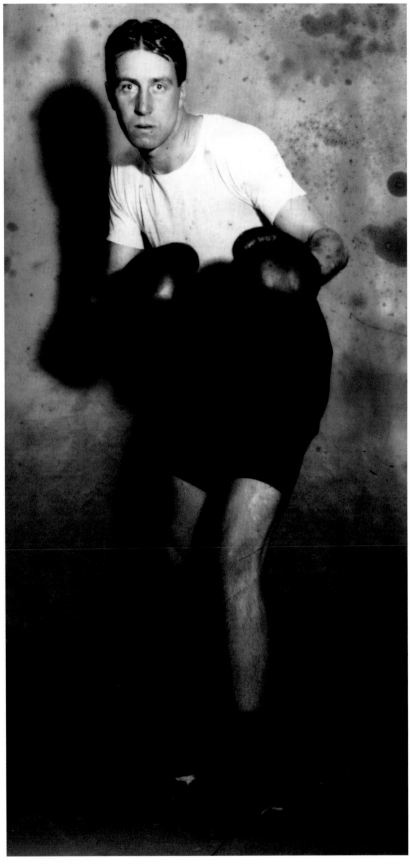

Olympic Middleweight champion and future England captain Johnny Douglas, four years before the first of his 23 Tests. 1908. Photographer not known

Opposite: Mike Gatting trains alone at Highbury football stadium. December 1980. Photograph by F. Tewkesbury/Evening Standard

Len Hutton (left) at an Army School of Physical Training. April 1940. Photograph by Fred Ramage/ Keystone

Taking a break at the Oval. August 1957. Photographer not known

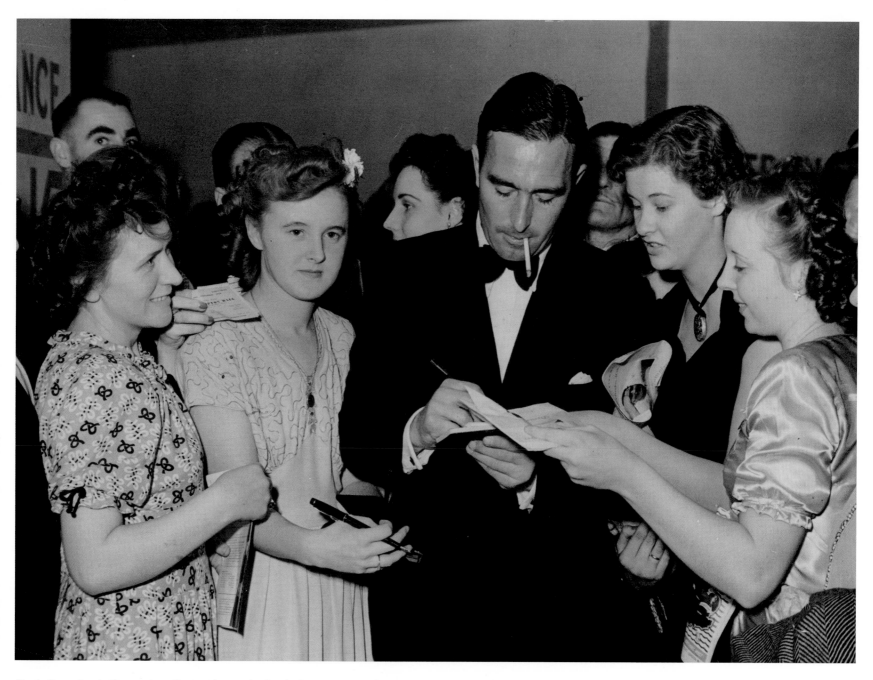

Denis Compton is the centre of attention at the Denis Compton Ball. October 1949. Photographer not known

Opposite: Walter Hammond, appointed captain of England for their forthcoming Ashes tour after 26 years in the game, takes stock at a county game between Gloucestershire and Leicestershire. August 1946. Photographer not known

Following pages, left: Scrambling to see at the Melbourne Cricket Ground. Date not known. Photographer not known

Following pages, right: A free view of the Gloucestershire versus All-India game at Cheltenham. August 1946. Photographer not known

Geoffrey Boycott, in bed with his bat. June 1989. Photograph by G. Davey

Opposite: Bedridden veterans of both world wars are given a prime view of the action for the Ashes Test at Melbourne. Circa 1946. Photographer not known

Cheltenham College cadets broadcast commentary from their cricket ground to 28 other schools on an inter-college link-up, organised by the army. July 1949.
Photographer not known

Opposite: John Arlott commentates on the Gloucestershire versus New Zealand game. August 1949. Photograph by Haywood Magee/Picture Post

The MCC depart Tilbury Docks for what would become
known as the Bodyline tour. September 1932.
Photograph by Davis

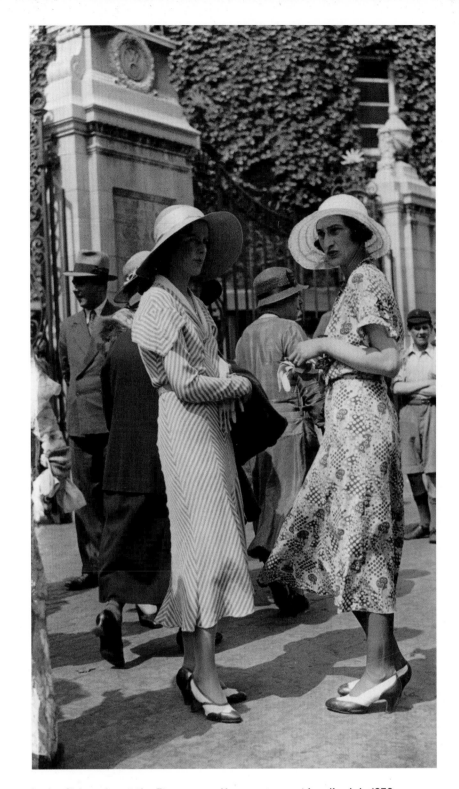

Lady aficionados at the Eton versus Harrow game at Lord's. July 1932.
Photograph by W.G. Phillips

Opposite: Spectators at the Eton versus Harrow game, Lord's. Circa 1905.
Photographer not known

Cricket on a Leeds wasteland. May 1953. Photograph by Carl Sutton

The immaculate works team of the Jaeger clothing company. July 1934.
Photograph by Sasha

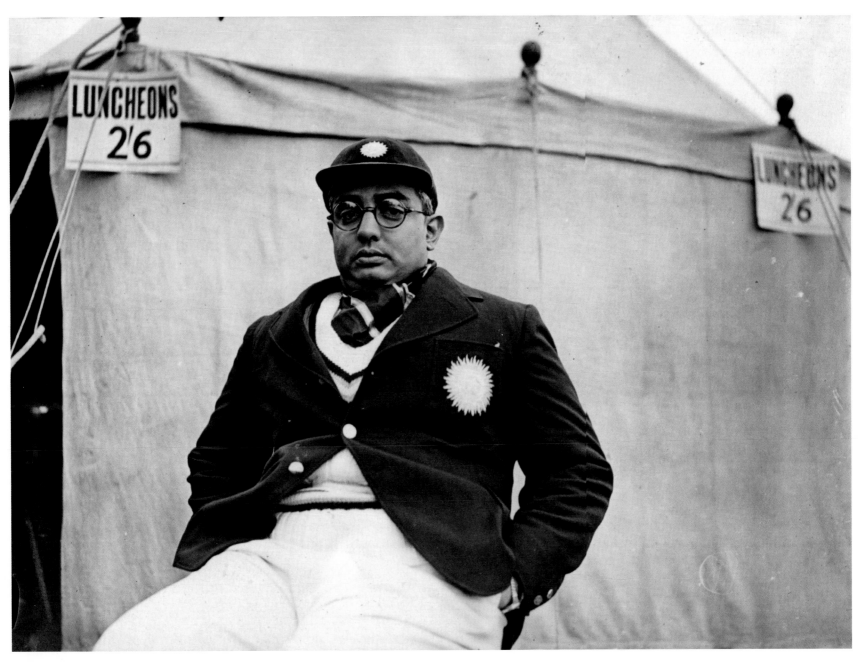

Vijaya Anand, the Maharajah of Vizianagram, captain of the All-India team. April 1936. Photograph by Hudson/Topical Press

Opposite: West Indies captain Clive Lloyd raises the first-ever World Cup, after an epic victory over Australia at Lord's. June 1975. Photographer not known

Games teacher, Marylebone, London. March 1934. Photographer not known

Opposite: Brian Clough bowls for the Lord's Taverners at Lord's. 1975. Photograph by Empics

England captain Freddie Brown. March 1951. Photographer not known

Opposite: Ex-England spinner Jim Laker shows his grip. March 1977. Photographer not known

Following pages: The new Kent Park ground, still under construction in Johannesburg. It will be ready for the MCC's visit in October. June 1956. Photographer not known

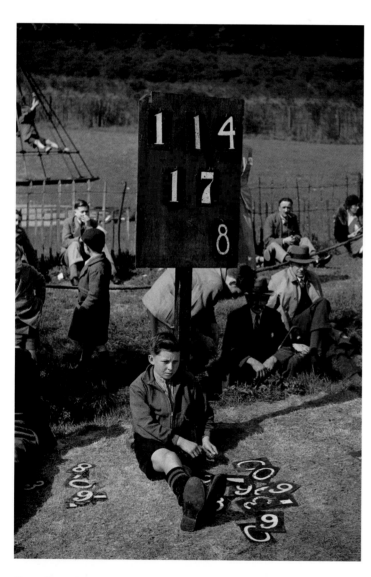

Scoreboard at the charity game between Surrey and Whyteleafe.
Circa 1940. Photographer not known

Opposite: Scoreboard at a local game on the Bombay Medan.
January 1982. Photograph by Adrian Murrell/Allsport

Don Bradman (right) in the Strand, London. 1938. Photographer not known

Having presented the London Speedway Cup to Wembley captain Bill Kitchen, Denis Compton rides pillion on a lap of honour. October 1949. Photographer not known

Opposite: Stuart Surridge (right) and Alan Moss set out to collect the willow harvest. The trees will be made into bats at Surridge's factory. March 1952. Photographs by Dennis Oulds

Australian vice-captain Jeff Thomson and his wife Cheryl model the latest fashions for an Australian chain store. March 1978. Photographer not known

Opposite: Modelling hand-knitted Burberry cricket sweater dresses. February 1966. Photograph by Reg Speller

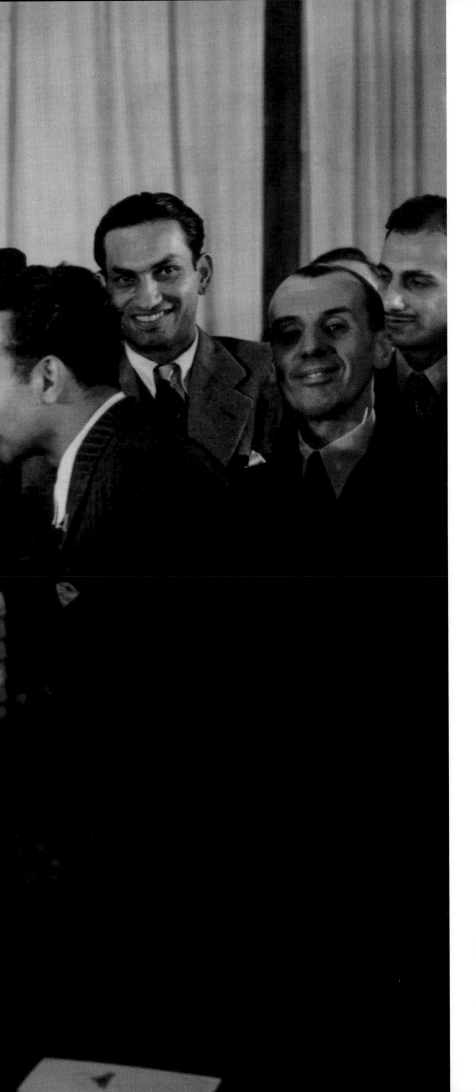

Actress Deborah Kerr presents vice-captain Vijay Merchant and the rest of the Indian team with state-of-the-art radios, on behalf of the Raymond Electric Company. September 1946. Photographer not known

Following pages: Supporters outside Edgbaston before the third England versus West Indies Test. July 1963. Photograph by Central Press

William Lewis tries out the seven-foot bat that is the prize in the annual challenge match between The Lamb and The Wolf public houses in Norwood Green, Middlesex. Photographer not known

Left: Merle Oberon and David Niven. Circa 1940. Photographer not known

England versus Australia, Trent Bridge: umpires Hardstaff (left) and Parry walk out. June 1930. Photographer not known

Opposite: Don Bradman in fancy dress. April 1938. Photographer not known

Above: The West Indies' Sonny Ramadhin at Cambridge. June 1950.
Photographer not known

Opposite: England cricketers take a break during filming at Pinewood Studios on the set of 'The Final Test'. The film stars Jack Warner and Robert Morley. From left to right: Alec Bedser, Cyril Washbrook, Denis Compton, Len Hutton, Richard Bebb, Jack Warner, Jim Laker, Godfrey Evans. November 1952.
Photographer not known

Cricket at St Moritz, Switzerland. February 1997.
Photograph by Mike Hewitt/Allsport

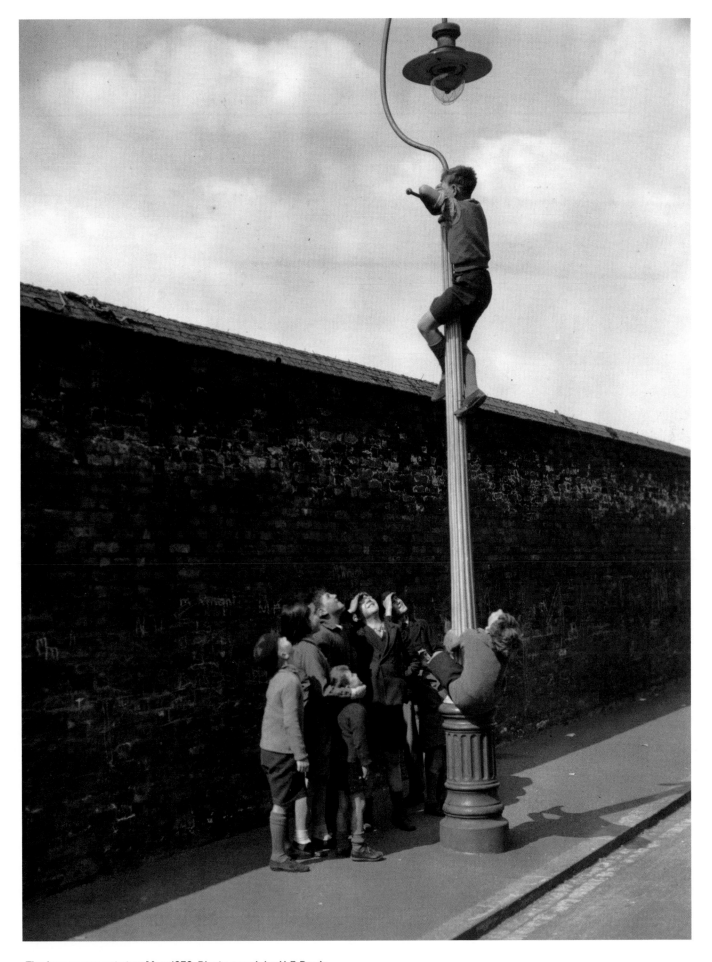

**The boy commentator. May 1938.** Photograph by H.F. Davis

**Opposite: Gas workers look for a lofty view of the Oval. July 1931.** Photographer not known

Australian slips in a line at Edgbaston. From left to right: Rick McCosker, Doug Walters, Greg Chappell, Ian Chappell. 1975. Photographer not known

Billy the kangaroo (right) takes a fresh guard at Manchester Zoo. 1929. Photographer not known

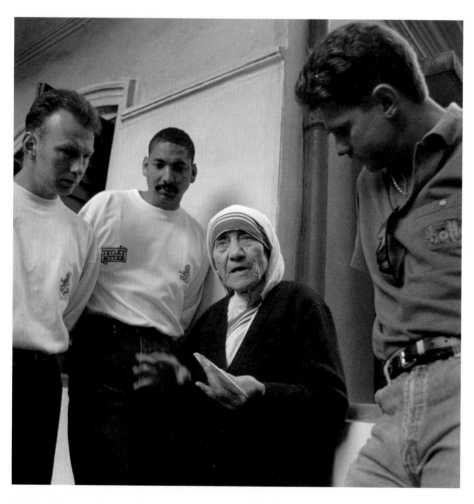

Mother Teresa of Calcutta advises England's Neil Fairbrother, Phil DeFreitas and Robin Smith in Calcutta on the perils of playing spin. January 1993.
Photograph by Chris Cole/Allsport

Opposite: Patsy Hendren demonstrates how to grip a ball. February 1936.
Photographer not known

The family and friends of British actor Jack Hulbert set an attacking field on the beach at Felpham, Sussex. August 1937. Photographer not known

Opposite: A short-lived variation on cricket named Vigaro – involving a tennis racket and six stumps – being played on Radlett Heath. July 1906. Photographer not known

Ex-England cricketer Maurice Tate pulls his first pint as landlord of the King's Arms, Rotherfield, Sussex. January 1950.
Photographer not known

Opposing captains the Duke of Norfolk and the Duke of Edinburgh before a game at Arundel Castle (Edinburgh bowled Norfolk for four). August 1953.
Photographer not known

Walking out for the traditional New Year's Day game at Hambledon. Date not known. Photographer not known

Don Bradman arrives for work. 1932. Photographer not known

Opposite: A worker at Warsop's the batmakers puts half-made blades out to mature. The company has taken record orders and will have 13,000 bats ready for the summer. April 1934. Photographer not known

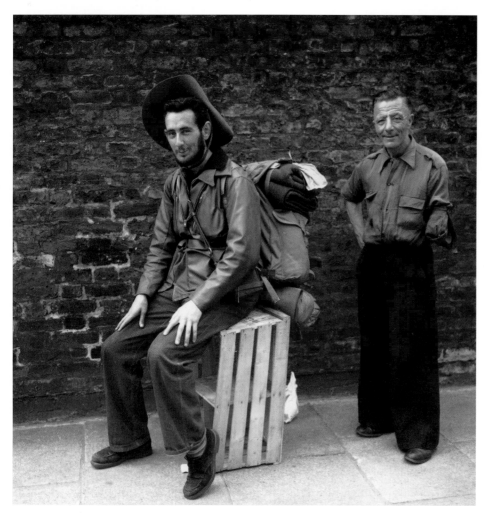

Aussie fan Jack Perry queues outside the Oval. He has been hitching round the country and seen four of the five Tests this summer. August 1953. Photograph by T. Marshall

Opposite: Convalescing soldiers watch a women's game at Hurlingham. July 1917. Photographer not known

Following pages: Hats and handkerchiefs at England versus New Zealand at the Oval. August 1949. Photographer not known

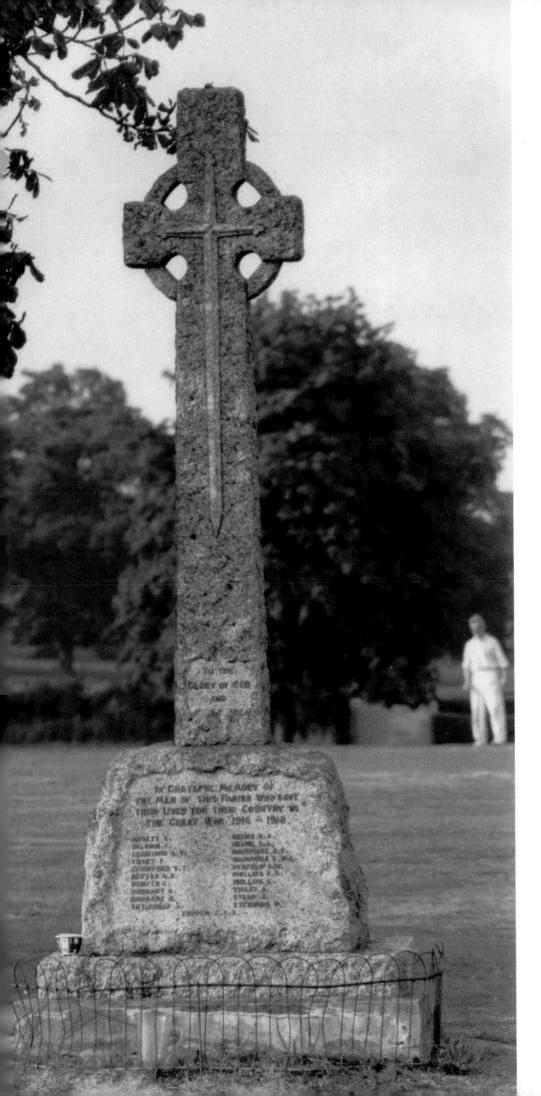

Village cricket, Wisborough Green, Sussex. September 1959.
Photographer not known

As England limp towards Ashes failure outside, Ian Botham prepares to make history at Headingley. July 1981. Photograph by Adrian Murrell/Allsport

Opposite: Peter Richardson in the dressing room at Worcester. May 1956. Photograph by John Pratt

The West Indies women's team practise at Lord's. June 1979. Photographer not known

Roedean girls learn the art of the forward defensive. June 1955. Photograph by L. Blandford/Harrison

Fourteen-year-old P.V. Davis who has made 324 runs in 8 innings and been offered a contract by Kent. June 1935. Photographer not known

Opposite: The Rego Ladies team listen to the yarns of veteran local haycutter Mr Wright at Edmonton, north London. May 1933.
Photograph by Reg Speller

Precarious standing room only at the Oval for England versus South Africa. 1929. Photographer not known

C.K. Nayudu (bottom left) visits London Zoo. 1930. Photographer not known

Opposite: At home with Maurice Tate. Circa 1930. Photographer not known

W.G. Grace with C.W. Alcock, the editor of 'Cricket' magazine. Circa 1900. Photographer not known

The West Indies' Learie Constantine and Wilton St Hill, on tour in England. 1928. Photographer not known.

Two holiday-makers turn out for a local team, to all-round amusement. August 1954. Photograph by Thurston Hopkins

Opposite: The MCC, about to fly to the West Indies. December 1953. Photograph by J.A. Hampton

Harold Larwood. 1927. Photographer not known

Opposite: England players during a rainbreak in the final Test of the series – they lead 3-0. From left to right : Geoff Miller, John Lever, Bob Willis, Graham Roope, Derek Randall. August 1977. Photograph by Graham Wood

Following pages: A Mexican wave of beer cans in Melbourne. December 1988. Photograph by David Cannon/Allsport

Dennis Lillee recuperates. June 1975. Photographer not known

Opposite: Comedy stalwarts Ian Carmichael (middle) and Brian Rix (right) with Alf Gover after a net at Gover's cricket school in Wandsworth, London. January 1970. Photographer not known

Voce, Mitchell and Larwood prepare for a fight, ahead of the Bodyline series. September 1932. Photographer not known

Opposite: Denis Compton and Godfrey Evans play golf on board the SS 'Stratheden'. 1950. Photographer not known

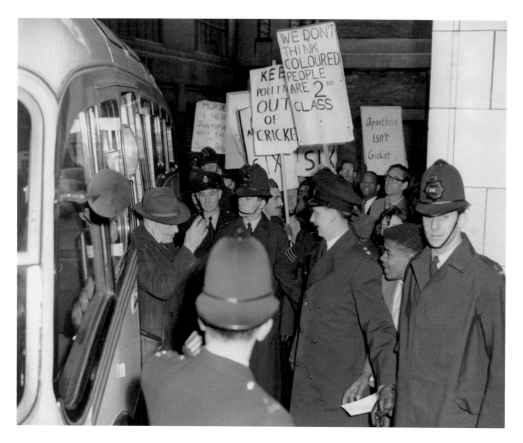

South African manager Dudley Nourse is greeted by protestors as the team arrives at the Park Lane Hotel at the start of their tour. April 1960. Photographer not known

Opposite: The Windsor Castle – the engine that pulled the Australian tourists' train from Paddington to Liverpool. Circa 1926. Photographer not known

Girls play cricket in the grounds of the Cadbury factory at Bourneville, Birmingham. July 1909. Photographer not known

Australia's Lindsay Hassett practises in Ceylon before a one-day match between Fremantle and Colombo. April 1938. Photographer not known

Opposite: Himalayan villagers. Circa 1894. Photograph by F.J. St Gore

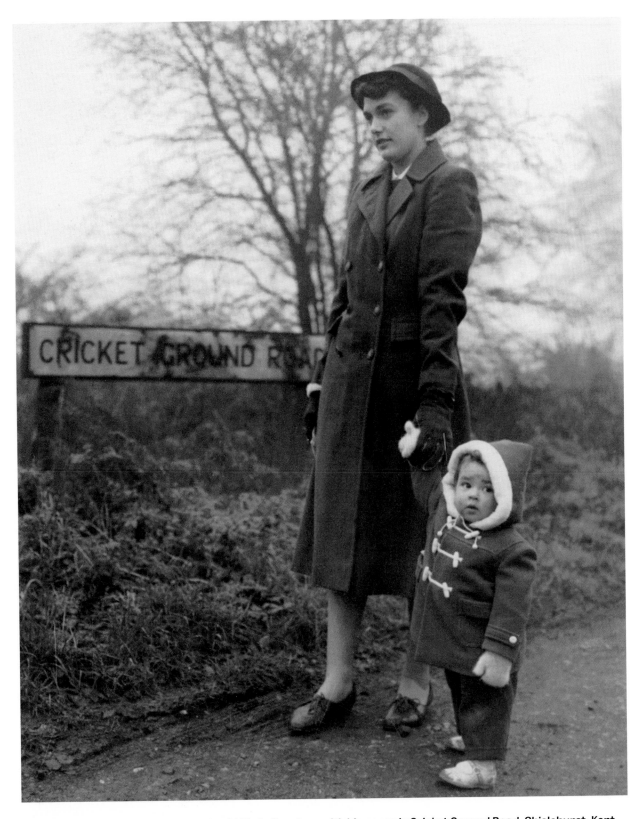

Christmas Eve: The fourteen-month-old Chris Cowdrey, with his nanny in Cricket Ground Road, Chislehurst, Kent. His mother has flown to Australia to be with his father, Colin, the England captain, for Christmas. 1958. Photograph by Keystone

Opposite: Richard and John Hutton, aged eight and five, listen for news of their father Len at home in Leeds, during England's tour of Australia. February 1951. Photographer not known

Mike Brearley and Bob Hope. March 1979. Photograph by C. Davey

Opposite: Denis Compton dances with Anna Neagle. October 1949. Photographer not known

Following pages, left: England and Yorkshire spinner Hedley Verity shows his bowling grip. April 1938. Photographer not known

Following pages, right: The grip that saw Jack Hobbs to a record 197 first-class centuries. Circa 1925. Photographer not known

A newspaper-seller brings the latest cricket news to London's Throgmorton Street. February 1920. Photographer not known

Street cricket near Regent's Park, London. July 1935. Photograph by Sasha

The South African embassy puts on a window display showing pictures of the England team, during the series between the two countries. July 1955. Photograph by Harrison

Opposite: Crowds gather on Brighton seafront to follow an illustrated scoreboard showing the latest from the Ashes Test at Lord's. June 1934. Photographer not known

Members of the Edmonton Cricket Club, north London, waiting to bat during a world record attempt at playing non-stop for a week. 1980.
Photographer not known

West Indies fans celebrate on the pitch at Lord's after seeing their team beat England by 326 runs. June 1950. Photograph by Sport and General/Empics

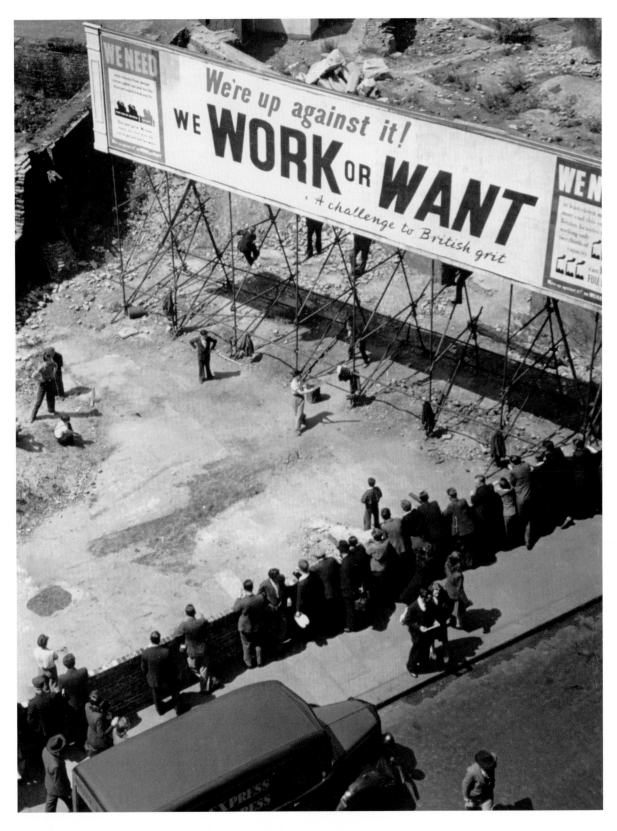

Bombsite cricket, London. Date not known. Photographer not known

Opposite: Street cricket in Millwall, London. August 1938. Photographer not known

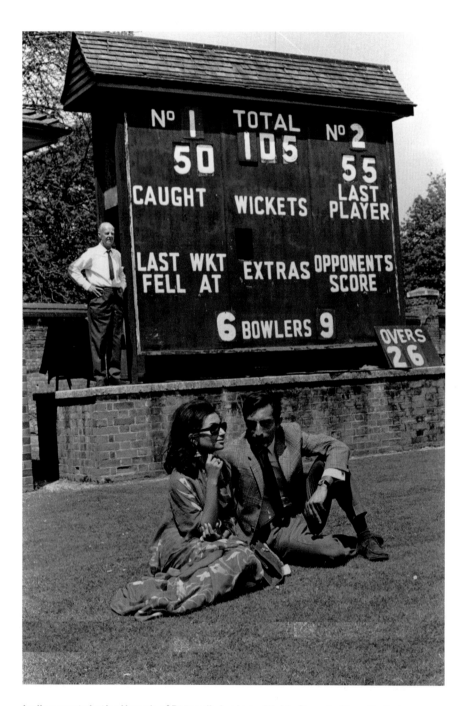

Indian captain the Nawab of Pataudi, Junior, with his fiancée Shamile Tagore. 1967. Photographer not known

Opposite: Village cricket in England. 1959. Photographer not known

Ian Botham gets ready for his professional football debut, for Scunthorpe Reserves.
March 1980. Photographer not known

Opposite: Denis Compton plays for Arsenal Reserves against Chelsea, at a packed Highbury
stadium. March 1948. Photograph by Ron Burton

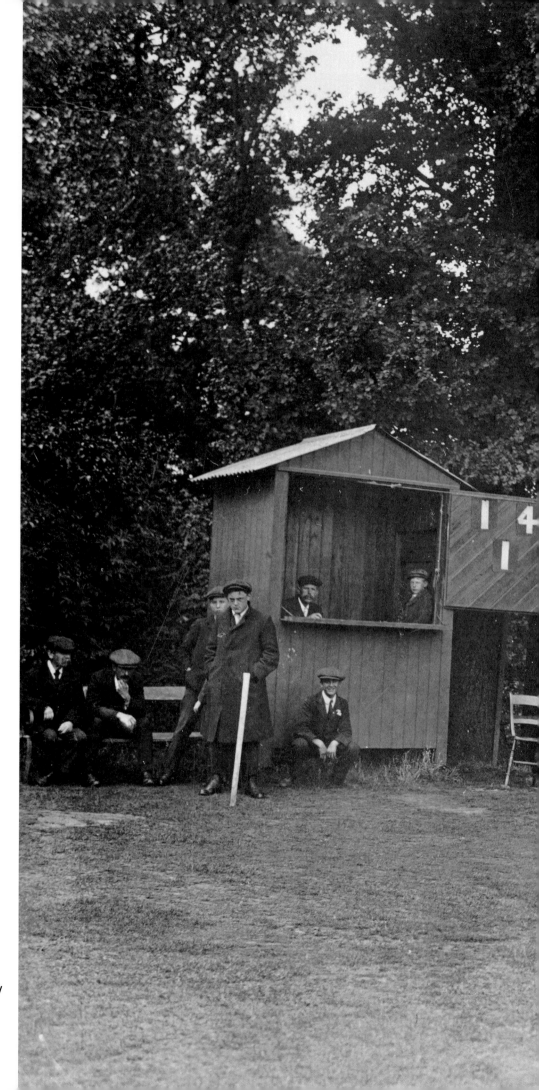

The pavilion at Sutton in Surrey – originally the town's railway station. August 1912. Photographer not known

The never publicity-shy ex-England captain 'Lord' Ted Dexter (right) promotes his forthcoming novel 'High Noon at Lord's', with co-author Clifford Makins. March 1975. Photographer not known

Opposite: Australia arrive in England. April 1912. Photographer not known

Boys from Westminster school watch a game between boarding and day pupils. Circa 1938. Photographer not known

Rolling the pitch at Vishkatapatnum, India, before the World Cup tie between Australia and Kenya. February 1996. Photograph by Shaun Botteril

Geoff Boycott takes over the decks from resident DJ Rusty Nails at Sydney nightspot Zoo. 1979. Photographer not known

Opposite: Detail of a new table-top cricket game. July 1948. Photograph by Bert Hardy

A Ladies XI against a Soldiers XI, with the servicemen dressed as pierrots. Circa 1918.
Photographer not known

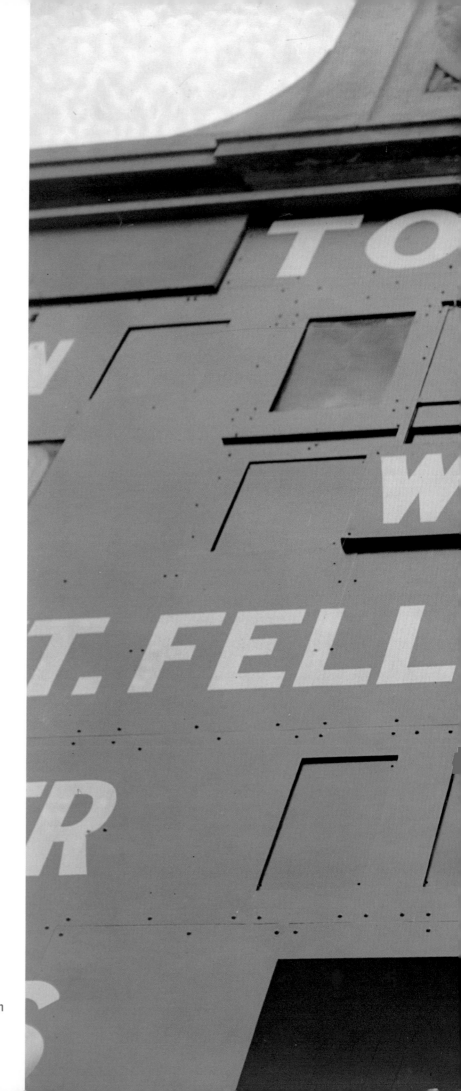

Cleaning the scoreboard at Hove, Sussex. April 1931. Photographer not known

England's Trevor Bailey films team-mates Colin Cowdrey, Frank Tyson and Denis Compton en route to South Africa. October 1956. Photograph by E. Bacon

Opposite: Early queuers, 8 a.m., Brisbane Cricket Ground. November 1946. Photographer not known

Spectators watch the Australian team in action in Colombo, Ceylon. April 1938. Photographer not known

Ian Botham on tour in India. 1981. Photographer not known

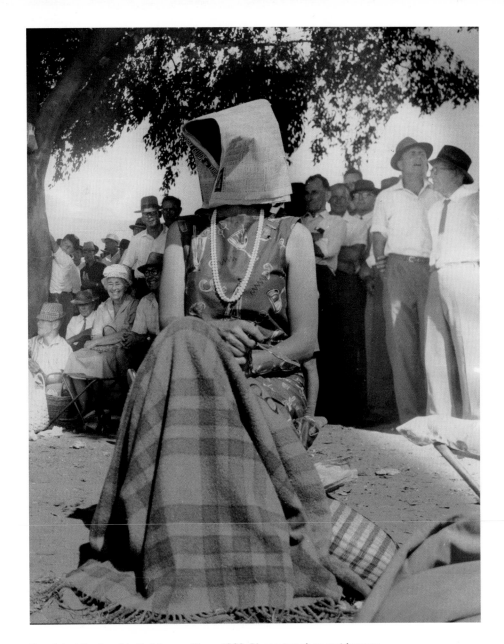

Surviving the heat in Brisbane. Circa 1962. Photographer not known

Opposite: Waiting for the rain to stop. Glamorgan versus Australia, Swansea. July 1938.
Photograph by Gerry Cranham

Preceding pages, left: W.G. Grace, photographed by a fellow Victorian cricketer. Circa
1900. Photograph by G.W. Beldam

Preceding pages, right: India's master spinner, Bishen Bedi, seen without his
trademark turban on India's tour of Australia. November 1977. Photographer not
known

Ex-England players at the launch of the Old England XI, which is to play a series of matches in aid of charity through the summer. From left to right: Derek Richardson, John Edrich, Godfrey Evans, Denis Compton, Fred Titmus, Fred Trueman. May 1981.
Photographer not known

Australia's cricketers, apparently delighted with their complimentary London Transport bus passes. August 1980. Photograph by Keystone

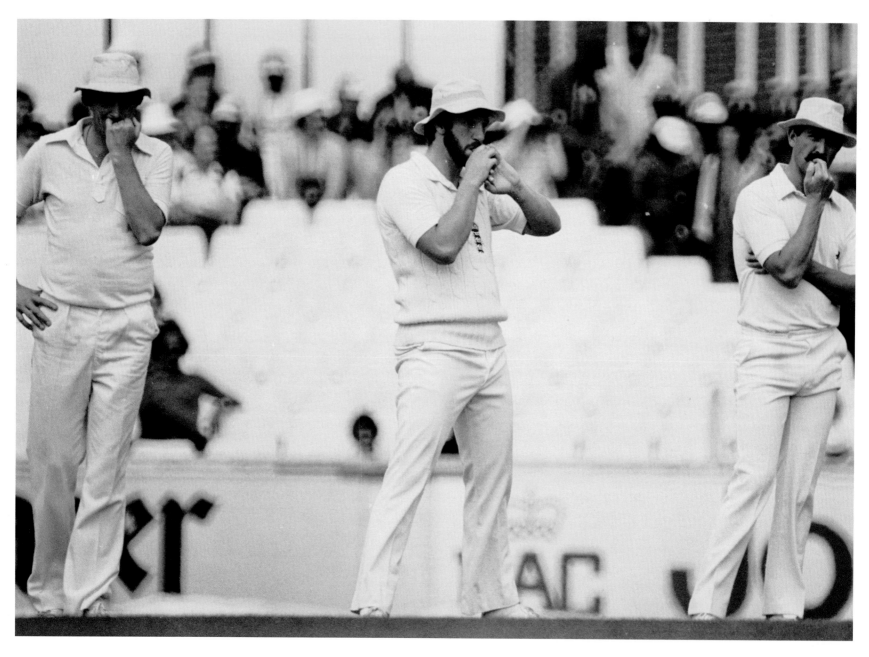

Nail-biting excitement for England's John Emburey, Ian Botham and Graham Gooch. July 1980. Photographer not known

Opposite: Len Hutton enjoys a rare post-war banana on arriving in Australia. October 1946. Photographer not known

Taking no chances ahead of a game of baseball in Oldham. May 1938. Photographer not known

Opposite: Former Australian opener Ian Davis demonstrates the extra protective gear he has designed ahead of facing the West Indies in a World Series Cricket game. 1978. Photographer not known

Elephant cricket at Skegness. September 1936.
Photographer not known

Joan Collins offers coaching advice to Bob Hope, while Bing Crosby keeps wicket in trademark laid-back fashion during the making of 'The Road to Hong Kong' at Shepperton Studios. July 1961. Photographer not known

Opposite: Fred Trueman, Pipeman of the Year, at the London Savoy to receive his award – a silver pipe. 1974. Photographer not known

Above: West Indies captain Garry Sobers congratulates Ray Illingworth after England clinch a series win at Headingley. July 1969. Photographer not known

Opposite: Australia arrive at Southampton. April 1938. Photographer not known

A game at the Scarborough Cricket Festival.
Circa 1913. Photographer not known

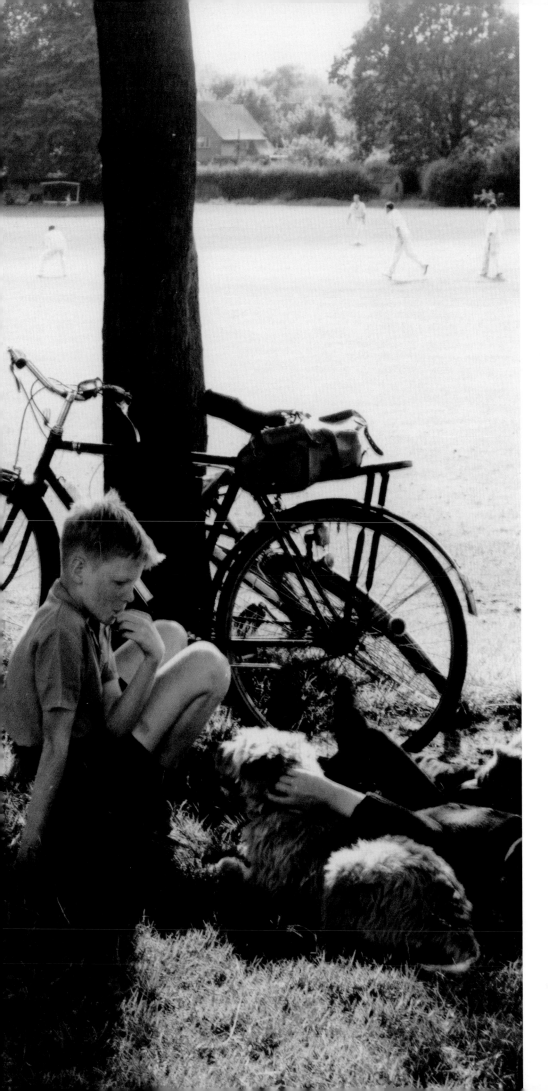

Village cricket, Oxted, Surrey. May 1966. Photographer not known

G.W. Beldam, noted sports photographer, Middlesex cricketer and inventor. Circa 1900.
Photographer not known

Opposite: Victor Trumper. 1899. Photograph by G.W. Beldam

Above: English garden party. August 1930. Photographer not known.

Opposite: South Africa arrive in high spirits at Southampton. April 1929.
Photograph by Davis/Topical Press

103-year-old William Capel takes to the wicket, with fellow residents of his Stratford residential home in the slips. Mr Capel is considered 'a marvel for his age' by doctors. June 1935. Photographer not known

D. Gregory of Australia. Circa 1905. Photograph by Reinhold Thiele

Opposite: Jack Hobbs sits for his Madame Tussauds model. 1930
Photographer not known

A young fan watches the second Australia versus West Indies Test from the top of the northern stand of the Melbourne Cricket Ground. January 1961.
Photographer not known

Opposite: Australian captain Richie Benaud. June 1961. Photograph by John Pratt

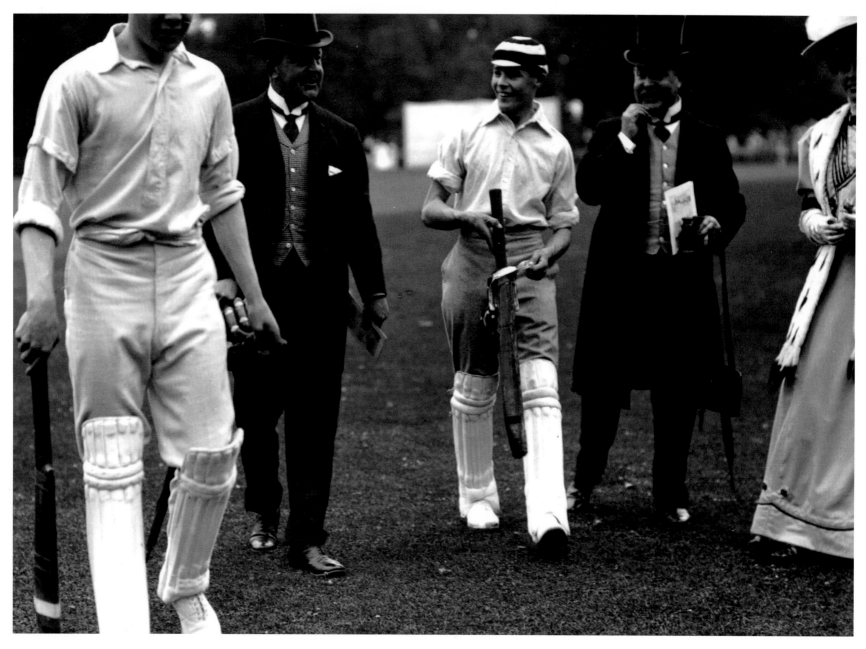

The Eton captain H.S. Hatfield (left) leads spectators to the pavilion. 1907. Photographer not known

Opposite: Spectators at Lord's. Circa 1905. Photograph by Reinhold Thiele

The New Zealand tourists visit Wookey Hole, Somerset. Circa 1933.
Photographer not known

An impromptu crowd greets a visit by Don Bradman to Sydney. December 1930. Photographer not known

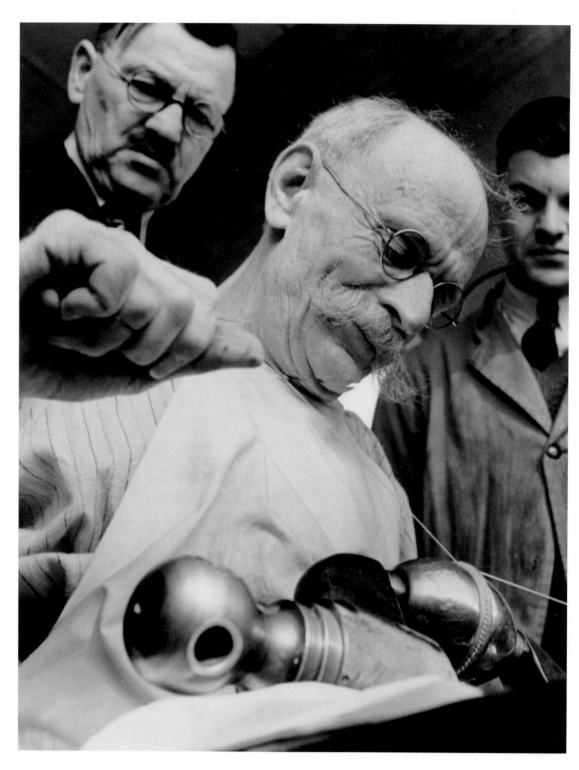

Stitching a cricket ball at the Reader factory, near Maidstone, Kent. February 1939.
Photographer not known

Opposite: Ken Munday, production manager of British Cricket Balls, tests the company's handmade balls, using a wind tunnel, to see how much each one is likely to swing. The measurement has no commercial or cricketing use at present, but it is hoped that in the future bowlers or captains may be able to choose balls according to their predetermined swingability. Circa 1975. Photographer not known

British Cricket Balls

Gracie Fields gets ready to appear for an Actors' XI, with help from fellow entertainers Sam Livesey (left) and Sir Gerald du Maurier. September 1929
Photographer not known

Opposite: Denis Compton with the Acton, Brentford and Chiswick schoolboys team, which has won the Compton football trophy. April 1952. Photographer not known

Australian selectors Jack Ryder (left) and Dudley Seddon, in Sydney, choose the team for the first Ashes Test in phone conference with Sir Donald Bradman, in Adelaide. November 1954. Photographer not known

Opposite: Brian Johnston ignores all generally accepted rules of safety to broadcast from his bath. May 1952. Photographer not known

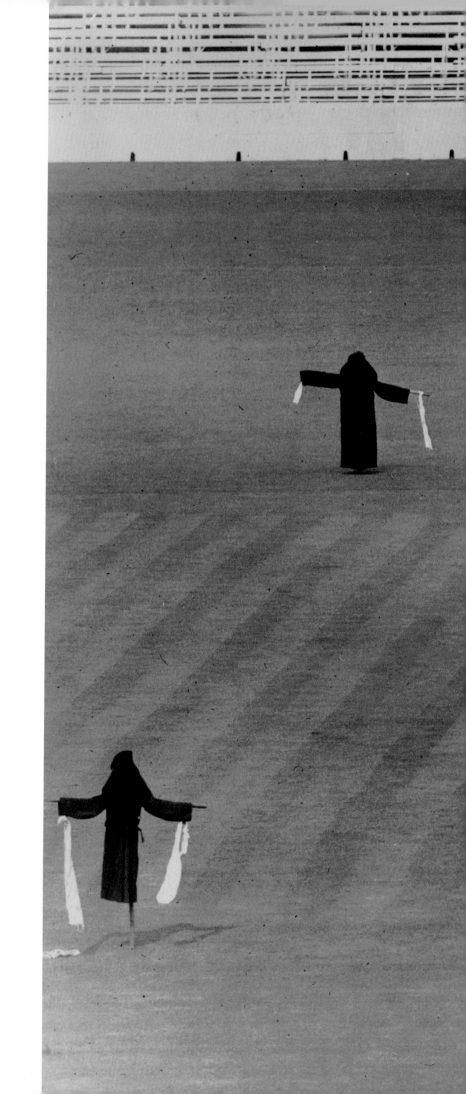

Surrey groundsman Bert Lock puts out scarecrows. April 1957.
Photographer not known

West Indies fans celebrate their win over
England at Lord's. August 1973.
Photograph by Leonard Burt

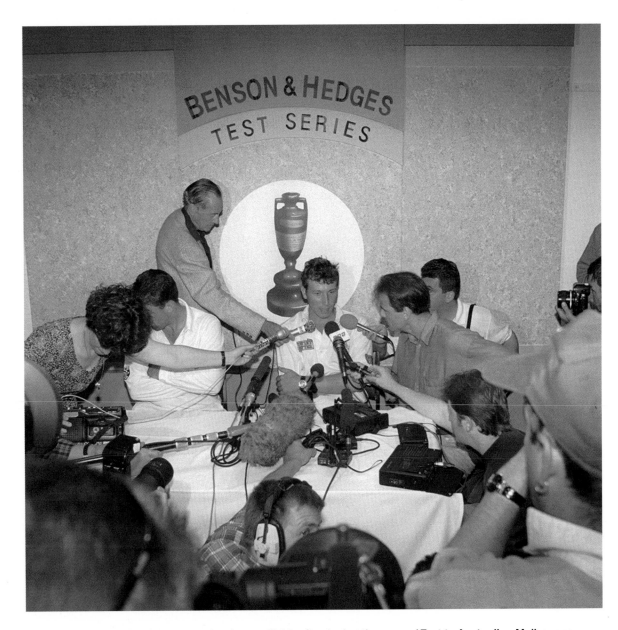

England captain Mike Atherton under the spotlight, after losing the second Test to Australian Melbourne. December 1994. Photograph by Graham Chadwick

Opposite: Neville Cardus addresses a dinner in honour of the touring West Indians. May 1950. Photographer not known

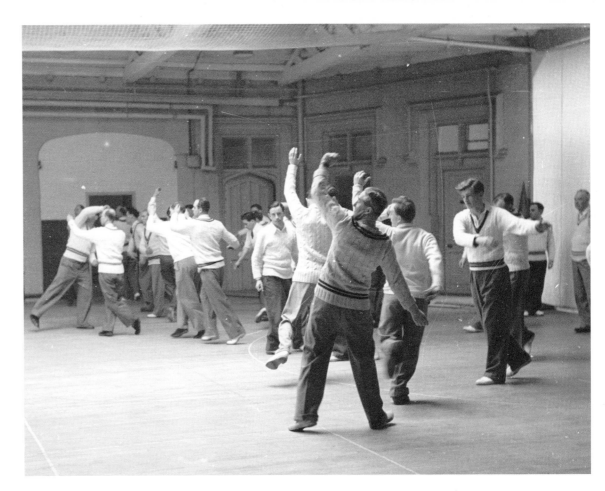

Learning to bowl, as part of 'Cricket for the Million', the MCC's new drive to promote the game more widely. May 1952. Photograph by Raymond Kleboe

Opposite: Teaching young players to play by the book at Loughborough. July 1945. Photograph by Haywood Magee

On the way to a coaching lesson in North Kensington Gardens. May 1939. Photographer not known

Opposite: A model wearing the body armour worn by Australian cricketers during the Bodyline series. December 1932. Photographer not known

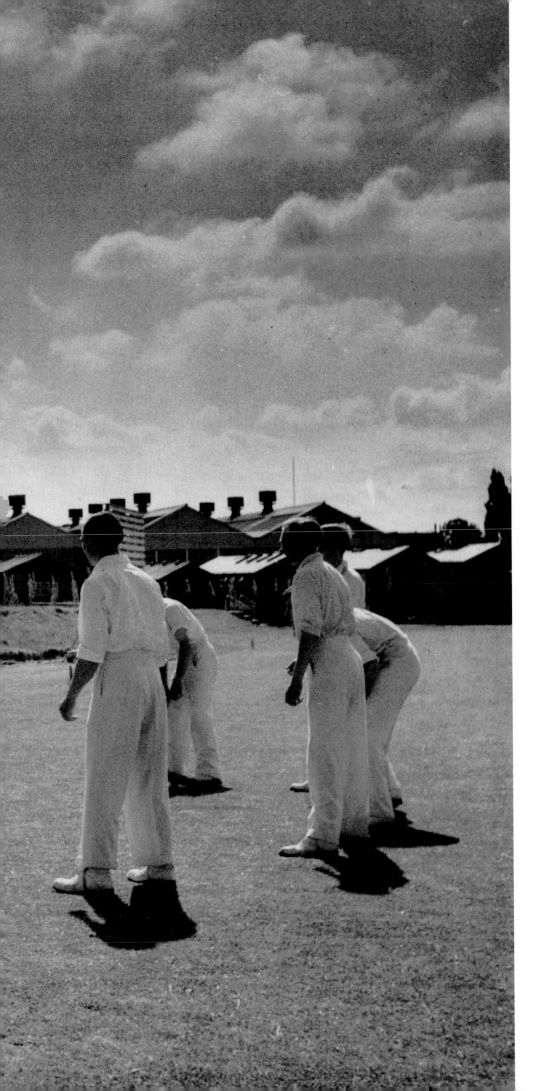

Practice for the British Timken works team. August 1952.
Photograph by Haywood Magee

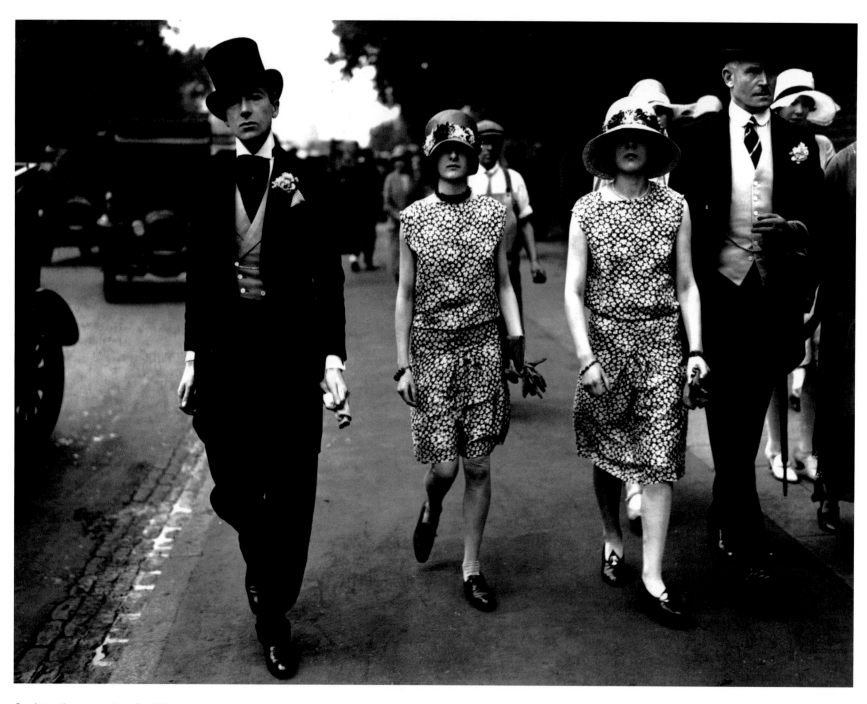

Society photographer Cecil Beaton arrives with his sisters for the Eton versus Harrow game at Lord's. Circa 1927. Photographer not known

New South Wales players with fashion guru Mal Clifford, who designed their new one-day kits, and his small dog. 1979. Photographer not known

A dandy at Lord's. August 1976. Photographer not known

Opposite: Somerset fan at Lord's for the Gillette Cup semi-final against Middlesex. August 1979.
Photograph by Tewkesbury

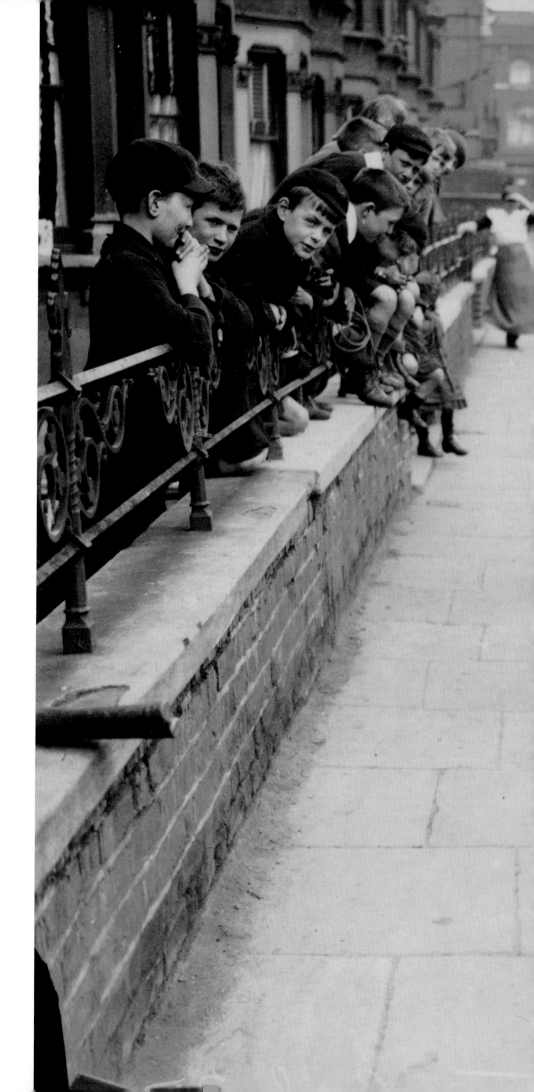

Street cricket, London. March 1926. Photographer not known

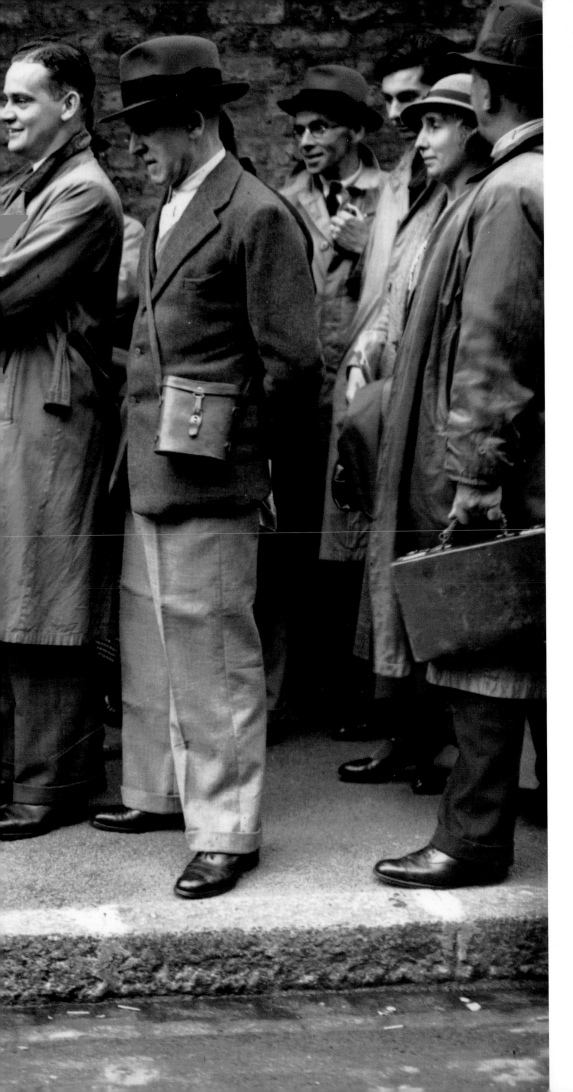

Listening to the radio in the queue outside the Oval.
August 1938. Photograph by Davis

Learie Constantine and Jack Hobbs share a joke over tea at a reception for the West Indies tour party in London. June 1939. Photographer not known

Opposite: India's Bishan Bedi and Australian captain Bobby Simpson, after India's innings victory at Sydney. January 1978. Photographer not known

Jack Russell returns to England's World Cup base in Peshawar, Pakistan. February 1996. Photograph by Chris Turvey/Empics

Opposite: Young cricketers in a newly pedestrianised street in Salford. April 1938. Photographer not known

353

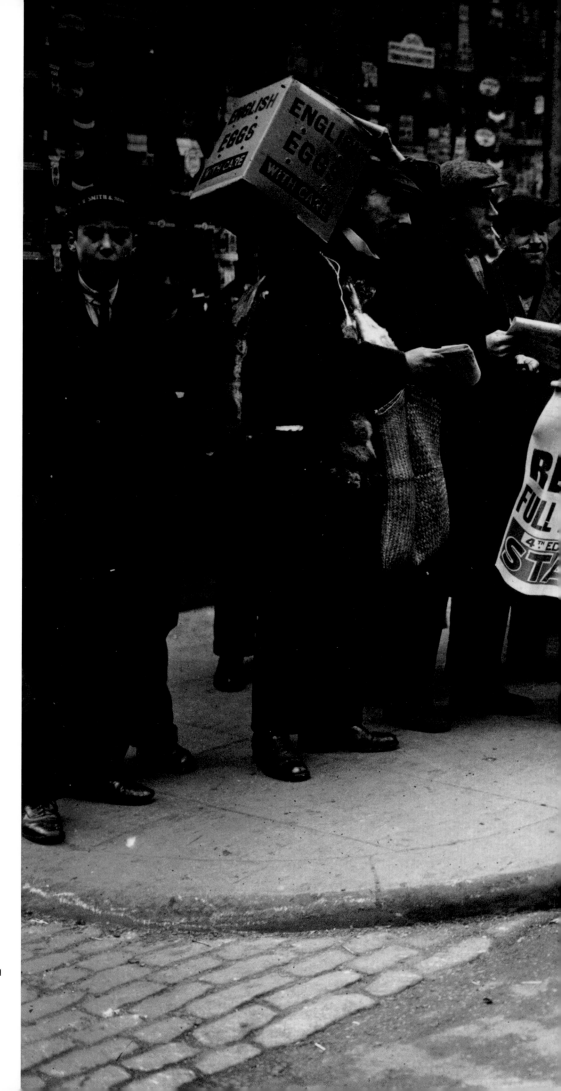

A newspaper-seller makes the most of England's victory in
the Bodyline series. February 1933.
Photograph by J.A. Hampton/Topical Press

England fail to present a united front ahead of the 1981 West Indies tour. January 1981. Photograph by Rob Taggart

A heatwave in England. Circa 1939. Photographer not known

Waiting for play to begin after a thunderstorm. The Parks, Oxford, June 1951. Photograph by William Vanderson

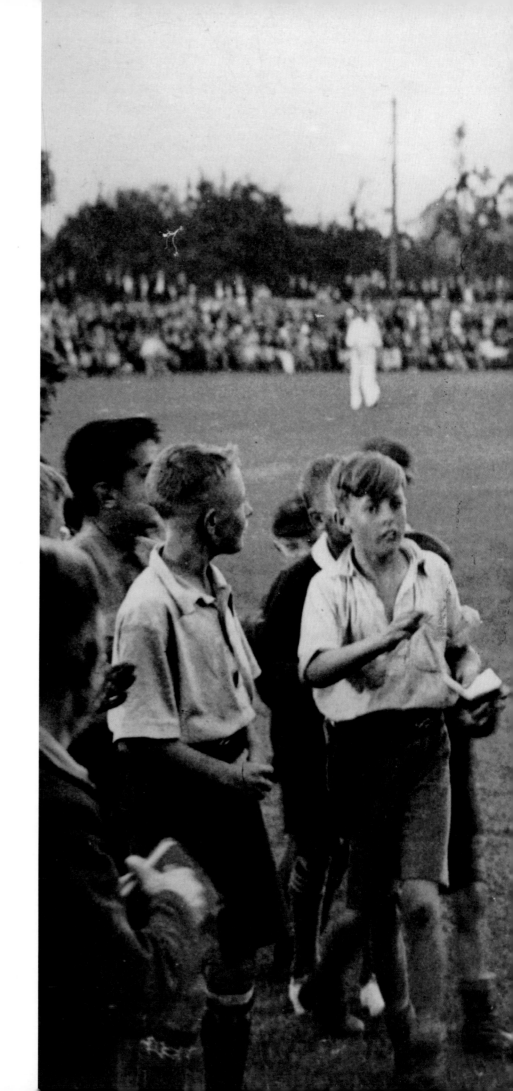

Walter Hammond returns to the pavilion at Bristol. August 1934.
Photographer not known

Fighter pilots get up a game between flying missions across the Channel to bomb the German frontline. June 1941. Photographer not known

363

A cricketer going out to bat whilst pushing a baby in a pram at the start of the match between Licensed Victuallers and Tradespeople at Dartford. June 1936. Photograph by E. Dean

Opposite: Joe Filliston, still umpiring club games every weekend at the age of 101. June 1962. Photographer not known

A cricketing wedding, Maresfield Church, Sussex, England. June 1930.  Photograph by J.A. Hampton/Topical Press

Opposite: Swollen joints on the spinning finger of the West Indies' Lance Gibbs. November 1968. Photographer not known

Eton schoolboys inspect bats. Circa 1926. Photographer not known

British-born Cary Grant brings cricket chic to Hollywood. 1934. Photographer not known

Opposite: Lavinia, Duchess of Norfolk, welcomes her select XI, under the captaincy of Tony Greig, and their opponents, the touring Australians, to Arundel Castle. 24th July 1977. Photographer not known

Mrs Jack Hobbs gets her eye in, on the sands at Margate. April 20 1925. Photograph by Brooke

All set for a game on the beach. May 12 1934. Photographer not known

Getting the news out from the Oval. 1933. Photographer not known

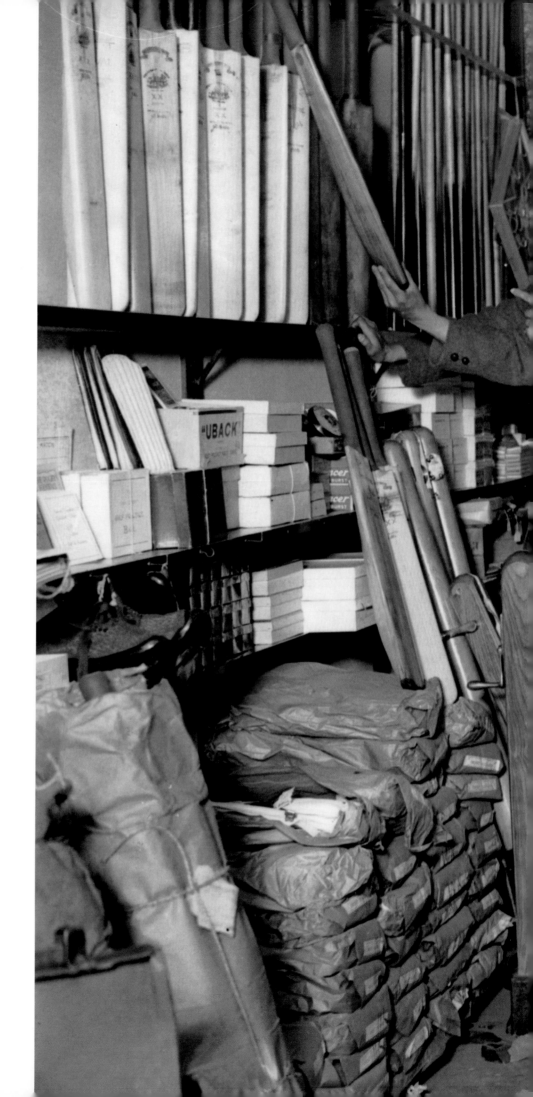

**Trying out bats inside Jack Hobbs' shop. July 1923.**
Photographer not known

The weapon of choice. July 1997. Photograph by Clive Mason

# INDEX

**A**

Acton, Brentford and Chiswick football XI: 326-327
Actors' XI: 149, 326
Addlestone 91
Alcock, C W 232
Alps, The 104
Amersham Hill 69
Angelow, Michael 117
Arlott, John 164
Arsenal 154-155, 268-269
Arundel Castle 212, 370-371
Ashes Song, The 20-21
Association of Cricket Ball Makers 128-129
Astill, W Ewart 51
Australia
    v England 1912: 272-273
    v England 1930: 42-43, 100-101, 196
    v England 1932-33: 243, 283, 338, 354-355
    v England 1934: 38, 258-259
    v England 1938: 18-19, 58, 59, 61, 67, 125, 302-303, 335, 348-349
    v England 1948: 56-57
    v England 1953: 12-13, 112-113
    v England 1954-55: 329
    v England 1972: 15
    v England 1977: 370-371
    v England 1980: 292-293
    v England 1981: 223
    v India 1977-78: 350-351
    v Sri Lanka 1975: 110-111
    v West Indies 1960-61: 317
    v West Indies 1968-69: 62-63
    v West Indies 1978: 296

**B**

baby in pram 364
ballmaking 102-103, 128-129, 139, 324, 325
baseball 297
bat, seven foot long 195
bath broadcast 328-329
batmaking 25, 34-35, 118-119, 186-187, 215
Bayley, Trevor 282
beach cricket 209, 372, 373
Beaton, Sir Cecil 342
Bebb, Richard 198-199
Bedi, Bishen S 287, 350-351
Bedser, Eric A 82
Bedser, Sir Alec V 82, 198-199
beer cans 62-63, 238-239
Beldam, G W 309
Benaud, Richard 316

billiards 51
boaters 68
Bodyline series 166-167, 243, 283, 338, 354-355
Bombay 183-183
bombsite cricket 10-11, 49, 265
Boon, David C 148
Botham, Ian T 86-87, 104, 105, 123, 223, 269, 285, 294, 344
Bournemouth Pier 130-131
Bourneville 246-247
Boycott, Geoffrey 123, 163, 276
Bradman, Sir Donald G
    before match 1932 214
    fancy dress 1938: 197
    Headingley 1938: 59
    injured at The Oval 1938: 58
    name used in protest 1948: 56-57
    Strand 1938: 184-185
    Sydney street crowd 1930: 322-323
    telephone conference 1954: 329
    toss 1938 67
Brearley, J Mike 253
Brighton 258-259
Brighton Foot Beagles 17
Brisbane 283, 289
Bristol 142-143, 360-361
British Cricket Balls 325
British Timken XI: 340-341
Broadhalfpenny Down 120-121
Brown, Freddie R 179
Buckingham Palace 54-55

**C**

Cadbury factory 246-247
Café Royal 85
Cambridge 199
Capel, William 312-313
Cardus, Sir Neville 334
Carmichael, Ian 240-241
centenarians
    'batting' 312-313
    umpiring 364-365
Chappell, Greg S 204
Chappell, Ian M 204
Charlton Athletic 107
Charlton, Bobby 84
Cheltenham 160
Cheltenham College 165
Chichester 147
Chislehurst 251
Church Times Cup 147
Clifford, Mal 343
Clough, Brian 177
coaching

batting 88-89, 336-337
bowling 337
coaches 88-89
schoolboys 339
Cobham 126
Cochrane, Mr and Mrs 25
Collins, Joan 300
Colombo 24, 284
commentators
    Arlott, John 164
    Cheltenham College cadets 165
    Jardine, Douglas R 38
    Johnston, Brian 20-21, 328-329
    Milburn, Colin 30-31
    schoolboy 203
Compton football trophy 326-327
Compton, Denis C S 12-13, 159, 186, 198-199, 242, 252, 268-269, 282, 290-291, 326-327
Constantine, Lord (Learie N) 233, 351
Cowdrey, Chris S 251
Cowdrey, Colin 282
Cowdrey, Lord (M Colin) 146
Cowell, Tim 48
Cricket Council, The 134-135
Cricket for the Million project 337
Cricket Ground Road 251
Crosby, Bing 300

**D**

Dad's Army (television) 152-153
Dartford 364
Davis, Ian 296
Davis, P V 227
day-night game 44-45
DeFreitas, Philip A J 206
Denis Compton Ball 159
Dexter, E R (Ted) 273
Douglas, J W H T (Johnny) 155
dressing rooms 142, 147, 222, 223
du Maurier, Sir Gerald 326
Duke and Sons 128-129
Durham 148

**E**

Edgbaston 192-193, 204
Edinburgh, HRH Duke of 94-95, 212
Edmonton 226-227, 260-261
Edrich, John H 290-291
Edrich, W J (Bill) 12-13
elephants 104, 298-299
Emburey, John E 294
England
    v Australia 1930: 42-43, 100-101, 196
    v Australia 1932-33: 166-167, 243,

283, 338, 354-355
  v Australia 1934: 38, 258-259
  v Australia 1938: 18-19, 58, 59, 61, 67, 125, 348-349
  v Australia 1948: 56-57
  v Australia 1953: 12-13, 112-113
  v Australia 1970-71: 20-21
  v Australia 1972: 15
  v Australia 1977: 236-237
  v Australia 1978-79: 86-87
  v Australia 1981: 223
  v New Zealand 1949: 218-219
  v South Africa 1929: 228-229
  v South Africa 1955: 258
  v South Africa 1956-57: 83
  v South Africa 1969: 134-135
  v Sri Lanka 1993: 76
  v West Indies 1950: 262-263
  v West Indies 1953-54: 234
  v West Indies 1963: 74, 192-193
  v West Indies 1969: 302
  v West Indies 1973: 75
  v West Indies 1980-81: 356-357
England football 84
England touring team to America 1859: 150-151
Eton 43, 97, 168-169, 318, 342, 368-369
Evans, T Godfrey 122, 198-199, 242, 290-291

**F**

Fairbrother, Neil H 206
fancy dress parties 83, 122, 123, 197
Felpham 209
Fields, Gracie 326
Filliston, Joe 364-365
Final Test, The (film) 132, 198-199
Fleet Street 22-23, 376-377
Fry, Charles B 50-51
funeral, W G Grace 114-115

**G**

garden parties 54-55, 311
Gatting, Mike W 154-155
Gibbs, Lance R 366
Glamorgan 288-289
Gloucestershire 142-143
Goddard, John 137
Gooch, Graham A 124, 294
Gover, Alf R 51, 240-241
Gower, David I 86-87
Grace, W G 114-115, 232, 286
Grant, Cary 370
Gregory, D W 314
Greig, A W (Tony) 370-371

**H**

Hambledon 120-121, 213
Hammond, W R (Wally) 67, 142-143, 158, 360-361
handicapped players 48
handkerchiefs as hats 218-219
Harben, Edward 149
Hardstaff, J senior 196
Harrow 43, 97, 168-169, 342
Hassett, A Lindsay 249
Hatfield, H S 318
hats 42-43, 68, 69, 96, 97, 218-219, 364
Headingley 42-43, 59, 125, 223
Heathrow Airport 92-93
Hendren, E H ('Patsy') 206-207
Hendrick, Mike 86-87
Heyhoe-Flint, Rachael 77
High Noon at Lord's (novel) 273
Highbury stadium 154-155, 268-269
Hill, Graham 82
Himalayan cricket 248-249
Hinwick Hall 48
Hobbs Gates, The 72-73
Hobbs, Lady (Mrs Jack) 372
Hobbs, Sir John B (Jack) 22-23, 34-35, 72-73, 255, 314-315, 351, 376-377
Holmes, Errol 98-99
Hope, Bob 253, 300
Hove 280-281
Hulbert, Jack 209
hunt 120-121
Hurlingham 32, 33, 216-217
Hurst, Geoff 85
Hutton, John 250
Hutton, Richard A 250
Hutton, Sir Leonard 61, 112-113, 132, 156, 198-199, 295

**I**

Illingworth, Ray 302
India
  v Australia 1977-178: 350-351
  v England 1932: 80-81

**J**

Jack Hobbs Ltd 22-23, 376-377
Jagger, Mick 15
Jaguar clothing XI: 172-173
Jardine, Douglas R 38, 51
Johannesburg 180-181
Johnson, Hophnie H H 137
Johnson, Mary 106-107
Johnston, Brian A 20-21, 328-329

**K**

kangaroo 205
Kenton 26
Kerr, Deborah 190-191
King's Arms public house 210-211
Kitchen, Bill 186
Knott, Alan P E 107

**L**

ladies' cricket
  Addlestone 91
  beach game 373
  Cadbury factory 246-247
  catches 91, 106-107
  first county match 46-47
  Heyhoe-Flint, Rachael 77
  holiday-makers 235
  Hurlingham 216-217
  Johnson, Mary 106-107
  make up 127
  Middlesex 46-47
  nurses XI: 144-145
  Rego XI: 226-227
  Roedean school 225
  smoker 98
  v Soldiers XI: 278-279
  West Indies XI: 224
  Women's Cricket Association 126
Laker, J C (Jim) 83, 178, 198-199
Lamb public house, The 194
Larwood, Harold 39, 236, 243
Lavinia, Duchess of Norfolk 370-371
Lawry, W M (Bill) 92-93
Leeds 170-171
Leicestershire 66
Lever, John K 236-237
Lewis, William 194
Lillee, Dennis K 241
Lillywhite, Freud and Co 70-71
Liverpool, Bishop of 146
Livesey, Jack 149
Livesey, Sam 326
Lloyd, Clive H 174
Lock, G A R (Tony) 18
Lock, H C (Bert) 330-331
London Speedway Cup 186
Lord's 43, 90, 97, 117, 168-169, 174, 224, 262-263. 319, 332-333, 344, 345
Lord's Taverners 77, 85, 177
Loughborough 336-337
lunchtime cricket 10-11, 49

**M**

Madame Tussauds 314-315
Makins, Clifford 273

Manchester zoo 205
marathon walk 105
Maresfield 367
Margate 372
Marsh, Rodney W 40
Marshall, Malcolm D 116
Martin, 'Bosser' 18-19, 67
Martin, Revd J 147
Mary, Arul 24
May, Peter B H 83, 146
McCormick, Revd W P 144-145
McCosker, Rick B 204
Melbourne 60, 160, 238-239, 317
Merchant, V M ('Vijay') 190-191
Mexican wave 238-239
Middlesex ladies 46-47
Milburn, Colin 30-31
Miller, Geoff 236-237
Millwall 264
Mitchell T B 243
modelling clothes 188, 189
Morecambe, Eric 82
Moss, Alan E 186-187
Mother Teresa 206
Munday, Ken 325

**N**
National Association of Groundsmen
    32, 33
Nayudu, C K 231
Neagle, Anna 252
New South Wales 343
New Year's Day 120-121, 213
New Zealand
    tourists c.1933 320-321
    v England 1949: 218-219
    newspaper sellers 256, 354-355
    non-stop playing record attempt
        260-261
Niven, David 194
Norfolk, Duke of 212
North Kensington Gardens 339
Norwood 100-101
Norwood Green 194
Nourse, A Dudley 244

**O**
Oberon, Merle 194
Old England XI: 290-291
Old Trafford 68
Oldham 297
Oval, Colombo 24
Oval, The 12-13, 15, 18-19, 36-37, 38, 53,
    58, 61, 65, 67, 72-73, 78-79, 100-101, 112-
    113, 157, 203, 218-219, 228-229, 330-

331, 374-375
Oxford 358-359
Oxted 306-307

**P**
Paddington station 244-245
Park Lane Hotel 244
Parks, The 358-359
Parry W R 196
Parsi touring team 1886: 140
Pataudi, Nawab of
    junior 133, 266
    senior 95
Penshurst Castle 98-99
Perry, Jack 216
Peshawar 353
Pinewood Studios 198-199
Pipeman of the Year 301
protective gear 296, 297, 338
protests and protesters 52, 53, 56-57,
    79, 110-111, 244

**R**
Radlett Heath 208-209
RAF cricketers 362-363
railway station into pavilion 270-271
rain 28-29, 288-289, 358-359
Ramadhin, 'Sonny' 199
Randall, Derek W 86-87, 236-237
Reader factory 324
Richards, Sir Viv 85
Richardson, Derek W 290-291
Richardson, Peter E 222
Rix, Brian 240-241
Road to Hong Kong, The (film) 300
Robinson, Cardew ('The Cad') 77
Roedean school 225
Roope, Graham R J 236-237
Rotherfield 210-211
Russell, R C (Jack) 353
Rusty Nails 276
Ryder, Jack 329

**S**
St Hill, Wilton H 233
St Moritz 200-201
Salford 352
Savoy Hotel 301
Scarborough 304-305
scarecrows 330-331
schoolboy cricket 170-171
schoolboy enthusiasts 374-375
scorers and scoreboards 266
    Bombay Medan 182-183
    Brighton seafront 258-259

    Bristol 52
    Hove 280-281
    Kenton 26
    Oval 18-19
    schoolboys' makeshift 374-375
Sydney 108-109
    Trent Bridge 27
    Westminster school 108
    Whyteleafe 182
Scunthorpe United 269
Seddon, C Dudley 329
Sheppard, Lord (David S, Bishop of
    Liverpool) 146
Shepperton Studios 300
Simpson, R B (Bobby) 350-351
Skegness 298-299
Smith, Robin 206
snow 148, 200-201
Sobers, Sir Garfield (Garry) 302
Somerset 14, 344
South Africa
    v England 1924: 66
    v England 1929: 228-229, 310-311
    v England 1955: 258
    v England 1960: 244
    v England 1970: 52, 53
South African embassy 258
Southampton 302-303, 310-311, 335
Southgate 147
spectators
    calypso celebration 262-263
    card-playing 36-37
    celebrating 75, 332-333
    Colombo 284
    Eton v Harrow 43, 97, 168-169, 342
    feet 64
    field invasion 76
    free view 160, 161
    hats 42-43, 68, 218-219
    Headingley 42-43
    heat 218-219, 289, 358
    Jagger, Mick 15
    Lord's 43, 97, 168-169, 319, 342
    not watching 157
    Oval, The, 1953: 12-13, 15, 100-101,
        112-113
    precarious views 65, 202, 203, 317
    queueing 36-37, 38, 192-193, 216,
        282, 348-349
    rain 28-29, 288-289, 358-359
    reactions 74
    schoolboy 97
    solitary 28-29, 108-109
    Somerset enthusiast 344
    standing 60, 160, 161, 228-229

streaker (female) 90
streaker (male) 117
Taunton 14
veterans 162-163
well dressed 345
Speedway 186
sponsorship 141, 236-237
Sri Lanka
    v Australia 1975: 110-111
    v England 1993: 76
Stewart, Mickey J 334-335
Stratford 312-313
Stratheden, SS 242
street cricket 257, 264, 346-347, 352
strikers 128-129
Surrey 141, 182
Surridge, W Stuart 186-187
Sutton 270-271
Swansea 288-289
swingability test 325
Sydney 39, 44-45, 62-63, 108-109, 276,
    322-323

**T**

table cricket games 86-87, 130-131, 277
Tagore, Shamile 266
Tate, Maurice W 17, 210-211, 230
Taunton 14
tea 124, 125
teacher (lady) 176
telephone exchange 136-137
Ten-pin bowling 83
tennis-cricket game 208-209
Thomson, Cheryl 188
Thomson, Jeff R 188
Throgmorton Street 256
tigers 231
Titmus, Fred J 290-291
Tonga 283
top hats 96, 97, 364
Trafalgar Square 144-145
training 16
Trent Bridge 27, 196
Trueman, Fred S 41, 152-153, 290-291, 301
Trumper, Victor T 308
turf-drying machine 32
turf-piercing machine 33
Tyson, Frank H ('Typhoon') 138, 282

**U**

umpires
    Amersham Hill 69
    centenarian 364-365
    England v Australia 1930: 196
    hats 69

**V**

Verity, Hedley 254
Victoria station 80-81
Vigaro 208-209
village cricket 220-221, 248-249, 266-
    267, 306-307
Vishkatapatnum (Indian ground) 275
Vizianagram, Maharajah of 175
Voce, W (Bill) 243

**W**

Walcott, Sir Clyde L 136-137
Walters, K Doug 204
Wandsworth 240-241
Warner, Jack 132, 198-199
Warsop's 215
wartime cricket
World War I 216-217, 278-279
World War II 362-363
Warwickshire 16
Washbrook, Cyril 198-199
weddings
    Cowdrey, Colin 146
    Maresfield 367
Weekes, Everton 137
West Indies
    v Australia 1960-61: 317
    v Australia 1968-69: 62-63
    v Australia 1975: 174
    v England 1939: 351
    v England 1950: 136-137, 262-263, 334
    v England 1963: 74, 192-193
    v England 1969: 302
    v England 1973: 75, 332-333
Westminster school 108, 274
Whyteleafe 182
Williams, Andy 334-335
Williams, Foffie 137
Willis, R G D (Bob) 86-87, 236-237
window display 258
Windsor Castle (locomotive) 244-245
Wisborough Green 220-221
Witham 118-119
Wolf public house, The 194
Wookey Hole 320-321
Worcester 222
World Cup
    1975: 110-111, 174
    1996: 353
Wright, Mr 226-227

**Z**

Zoos
    London 231
    Manchester 205

# PICTURE CREDITS

All pictures courtesy of Getty Images with the following exceptions:
Empics: 262-263, 353, 78, 177
Ramuchandra Guha: 140, 231, 248

# ACKNOWLEDGEMENTS

Special thanks to Ali Khoja for his unbeatable knowledge of the Getty
archives and help with picture research on this project; to Charles Merullo,
Liz Ihre and the rest of the Publishing Projects Department at Getty Images;
to Barbara Saulini for design; to Ian Crane for the index; to Barbara Dixon
and Roderick Easdale for proofing; to Katie Cowan for making sure things got
done; to Ray Steer, the veteran mystery bowler and county diehard who got
me interested in the first place; and to Claire Wills, the summer game's
newest and most passionate convert.